VERY ENTERTAINING

MENUS FOR SPECIAL OCCASIONS

....

BY
DIANE MORGAN
DAN & KATHLEEN TAGGART
GEORGIA VARELDZIS

Designed by
PATRICIA ZAHLER

Photography By
JERRY LAROCCA

Illustrations By
GAIL K. SONES

Edited By
LYNN LUSTBERG
DIANE MORGAN

PUBLISHED BY ENTERTAINING PEOPLE
PORTLAND, OREGON
1990

Library of Congress Catalogue Card Number: 89-81843

ISBN 0-9620937-1-8

Printed in Korea through Overseas Printing Corporation

Published by Entertaining People
17080 SW Arkenstone Drive
Durham, Oregon 97224

ALSO BY DIANE MORGAN, DAN & KATHLEEN TAGGART, AND GEORGIA VARELDZIS

ENTERTAINING PEOPLE
MENUS FROM A PACIFIC NORTHWEST COOKING SCHOOL
(Entertaining People, 1989)

Dedication

We dedicate this book to our families and to you,
our friends, out there—dedicated cooks and foodies all
—who have supported and encouraged us by
your enthusiastic acceptance and praise of our first book,
ENTERTAINING PEOPLE. You are the reason for
this second effort and we are most appreciative
of your support.

ACKNOWLEDGMENTS

Marianne Barber. As in our first book, Marianne was our most loyal recipe tester. Her comments, sent on sheets of steno paper, were invaluable.

CHASE LTD. Lynn Chase provided pieces of her stunning new dinnerware for our Christmas and Bridal Luncheon photographs. A dinner plate, in the Winter Game Birds pattern, graced our Christmas table. The Costa Azzura pattern of china and accessories brightened our Bridal luncheon.

Mary Donnally. Mary, a superb baker and cook, came through in a pinch when Kathleen was struggling to work out an egg white-based buttercream for the wedding cake. Mary's successful and delicious results can be found in the wedding menu.

Jane Foley. Jane is among the most skilled cake decorators we have encountered. For this reason, we asked her to make and decorate the cake for our wedding photograph. The beautiful result is evident herein.

Lynne and Nick Greve. The driving forces behind Carl Greve Jewelers and Gift Department, Lynne and Nick have provided constant support and encouragement. Their taste is impeccable and has influenced our tabletop designs significantly.

Cheryl Jackson and Dan Koch. Cheryl and Dan are the owners of Silver Plume Imports which brings from India some of the finest saffron available, as well as the wonderful props that enhance the Memories of India photograph.

Greg Morgan. Greg is our resident taster, critic, and whiz at the personal computer. Our hassles with word processing, disk conversions, and other computer headaches were easily solved by Greg.

Audrey Lieberman Murnaghan. Audrey was our co-author on Book One, and she still cares deeply about the quality, taste, and balance of our menus. She tested recipes energetically in the midst of a very busy personal schedule in Vancouver B.C., where she now resides.

TABLE OF CONTENTS

INTRODUCTION

VERY ENTERTAINING was conceived in late October of 1987 as the leaves in the Pacific Northwest turned red and gold. The promise of winter was in the air, carved pumpkins kept silent watch over trick-or-treaters and sunny skies gave way to clouds and drizzle. But for a group of five cooks there was a spring-like promise in the air—their first book, ENTERTAINING PEOPLE, was due from the printer in a few days. After two years of cooking and writing, the new authors were about to be rewarded with a cookbook of great color and style. ENTERTAINING PEOPLE was sold in Oregon and Washington at first, then came national distribution which required a second printing. The authors were still the same humble cooks they had always been, but now they were filled with pride. Thousands of people were enjoying reading and cooking from their award-winning cookbook. They began writing this, their second cookbook, almost at once.

VERY ENTERTAINING is brought to you by four souls who simply love to cook. They are absolutely unable to "just say no" when the opportunity to cook presents itself. These four friends share a common and constant desire to do with food what carpenters do with wood—create something of substance and beauty. Like others similarly afflicted, they have developed what could be called kitchen imagination, that unique ability to create flavorful and attractive dishes from whatever ingredients happen to be around. It is the kind of vision that sees a refrigerator groaning with leftovers and artfully *assembles them into a beautiful and substantial meal. For example, "Salad for dinner?" becomes romaine leaves topped with thin slices of red onion, slivers of cold leftover grilled beef, chunks of cold potato, ribbons of sweet red pepper, crisp tender cold cooked green beans, wedges of late-summer tomatoes, and sprinklings of Parmigiano-Reggiano napped with a vinaigrette of sherry vinegar, fresh rosemary, and extra virgin olive oil.*

Many of the menus in this book are the result of considering possibilities, the "what ifs." What if fresh leg of pork is given the cure of a master and a year hanging in cool, dry air? Prosciutto! What if a jalapeño is smoke-dried until it resembles a mummified pepper? Chile Chipotle! What if goat's milk is provided to a good cheesemaker? Chevre! (All right, goat cheese.) What if cumin is used in a yogurt dressing, what if cinnamon is stirred into a vinaigrette, what if saffron is cooked in a beurre blanc? Curiosity in the kitchen leads to ever more exciting cooking excursions. If a cook salivates just thinking of a fresh baguette, then imagine his pleasure in discovering that a topless pizza can be drizzled with olive oil, sprinkled with coarse salt and fresh herbs, and baked in a hot oven to become a mouth-watering focaccia! If a cook grew up in a family in which black pepper was considered hot (and maybe exotic), imagine her joy in trying cumin, black mustard seed, asafetida, and saffron.

VERY ENTERTAINING is more than a sum of its culinary parts, though. It reflects the authors' eagerness to invent occasions for which menus can be designed! Bowl Day Bash, for instance, includes everything from a layered fajita salad to beer-poached shrimp with Cajun mayonnaise. Indulgence is a dessert buffet including chocolate cheesecake, berry banana trifle, irresistible baklava, triple chocolate pastry nut balls, and more! Starting Over is a tongue-in-cheek "celebration" menu for the newly divorced featuring refried beans, twice-cooked pork, double baked potatoes and rhubarb upside down cake. New Year's Resolution contains two menus with reduced fat and low calorie dishes including curried cauliflower soup, oriental seared beef with vegetables, and a ricotta and lingonberry chocolate dacquoise. Between the covers of this book are 20 fresh and interesting menus, enough to keep the most confirmed cooking fanatics busy for at least a few days!

These four authors love to cook, and they also have a knack for presenting their foods in style. The settings photographed here are as warm and varied as the foods themselves. Each author has spent considerable time entertaining groups of adults during cooking classes (hence the ENTERTAINING PEOPLE title on the first book), and wanted his or her food photographed in an inviting and fun way. Thanks to graphic designer Patricia Zahler and photographer Jerry LaRocca, the authors' foods look VERY ENTERTAINING. This book is as fun to look at as it is to cook from!

VERY ENTERTAINING is meant to be used. Grease-stained and dog-eared cookbooks—even one this beautiful—are evidence of cooking enjoyment. The authors love nothing more than to be handed a tattered copy of their book for autographing. Their recipe writing and insistence on beautiful photography are nothing more than simple encouragement for you, gentle reader, to get out your chopping board and reach for your favorite kitchen knife...again, because life is too short for dull food!

Dan Taggart

Kathleen Taggart

Diane J Morgan

Georgia M. Vareldzis

FIRESIDE DINNER

We purposely kept this menu simple. If I want to serve a dinner by the fire, the last thing I need is a bunch of courses to keep me in the kitchen. What's nice about this menu is that most of the preparation can be done ahead of time.

Silky Two-Potato Soup

•

Almost Traditional Hungarian Stuffed Peppers

•

Maple Poached Pears on Chocolate Biscuits

I like to serve the soup while the conversation is young and the fire is just beginning to glow. Since the soup is a purée, it's perfect for serving in hefty mugs. The peppers make for great lap food, requiring only a fork and napkin. And the dessert, served with a steaming mug of coffee or cappuccino, nicely rounds out the meal as the fire turns to embers.

Dan's Silky Two-Potato Soup is truly inspired. It won rave reviews from all of us, his toughest critics, without even the suggestion of an ingredient change! I have made it on several occasions for my family, serving it with a green salad as a simple dinner. Even the leftovers are great.

The Almost Traditional Hungarian Stuffed Peppers have their heritage from my cooking days at The FarmHouse in Port Townsend, Washington. There we used the more traditional green peppers, but I prefer using red peppers for their color. I sometimes think my family roots should have been Hungarian instead of German and Lithuanian, because my love of the Hungarian spices as used in this recipe is so strong. When I smell onions and paprika sautéing in a pan, my appetite quickens and my fork is ready to dig in!

Kathleen, in her dedication to finding something to do with chocolate, married Maple Poached Pears and Chocolate Biscuits for a fanciful dessert. These are fun to make and fun to eat, and I particularly like the leftovers, if any, for breakfast!

This menu really calls for some dark beer or ale. In the Northwest, we have so many micro-breweries that I like to offer my guests a selection. Two particular favorites are Widmer and Henry Weinhard Ale. Why not take advantage of this occasion to try something from your neck of the woods.

Diane f Morgan

SILKY TWO POTATO SOUP

In a medium saucepan, melt the butter and sauté the onion, mushrooms, and parsley until they are soft but not brown. Add the stock or broth, potatoes, thyme, bay leaf, and worcestershire. Bring the soup to a boil, reduce to a simmer, and cook until the potatoes are tender, probably about 10 to 15 minutes.

Strain the soup, reserving the liquids in a large bowl. Purée the solids in a food processor or blender, adding as much liquid as is necessary to allow the mixture to move in the machine. Return the puréed mixture and remaining liquid to the pan and stir to blend.

Add the cream. Taste for salt and add as much as you think best. Add pepper to taste. When the soup is nearly simmering, portion it into bowls or a warmed tureen. Top with the chopped parsley or sliced scallions and serve. This is a hearty soup so portions need not be huge!

Serves 8.

4 tablespoons unsalted butter

1 medium onion, coarsely chopped

3 large mushrooms, coarsely chopped

1/2 cup tightly packed parsley leaves, chopped

6 cups good quality stock or broth

1 pound sweet potatoes, peeled, cut into 1-inch pieces

1 pound waxy potatoes, peeled, cut into 1-inch pieces

1/2 teaspoon dried thyme

1 bay leaf

1 tablespoon worcestershire sauce

1 cup heavy cream

Coarse salt and freshly ground black pepper, to taste

Chopped parsley or thinly sliced scallions for garnish

8 medium, sweet red peppers
....
3 tablespoons oil, divided
1 1/4 pounds lean ground beef
2 medium onions, chopped
1 tablespoon Hungarian sweet paprika
1 teaspoon Hungarian hot paprika
1/2 teaspoon ground cloves
1 15 1/2-ounce can tomato sauce
1 tablespoon caraway seeds
1 1-pound jar or package sauerkraut, drained, rinsed and squeezed dry
1/3 cup uncooked white rice
1 1/2 teaspoons coarse salt
1 teaspoon sugar
Freshly ground black pepper, to taste
....
1 1/2 cups sour cream
4 tablespoons whipping cream
Freshly minced parsley (optional)

ALMOST TRADITIONAL HUNGARIAN STUFFED PEPPERS

Cut the peppers in half lengthwise, remove the core and seeds. Reserve until ready to stuff. In a large sauté pan, heat 1 tablespoon of the oil. Add the ground beef and brown. With a slotted spoon remove the beef to a plate and reserve. Drain the fat from the pan.

Preheat the oven to 350 degrees.

Add 2 tablespoons of oil to the pan and heat. Add the onions and sauté, covered, for about 4 minutes, or until the onions are soft but not browned. Add the paprikas and cloves and sauté briefly. Add the browned meat and the rest of the ingredients and let simmer, covered, for an additional 10 minutes. Taste and adjust the seasonings.

Stuff the prepared peppers. Place in one large or two medium baking dishes. Spoon 1 tablespoon of water over the top of each pepper. Bake, covered, for about 1 hour or until the peppers are tender.

To serve, mix together the sour cream and cream until smooth and creamy. Place 2 generous tablespoons of the cream mixture on the bottom of each entree plate and spread with the back of a spoon to make a pool of cream. Place two pepper halves on each plate, sprinkle some minced parsley on top, if desired, and serve.

Serves 8.

DM

MAPLE POACHED PEARS ON CHOCOLATE BISCUITS

Place the pears in a 2 1/2 to 3 quart saucepan with the water, maple syrup, and lemon juice. Bring mixture to a simmer and poach until tender when pierced with a fork. This will take about 10 minutes for medium-ripe pears and 15 minutes for firm ones.

When the pears are tender, remove with a slotted spoon. Reduce the poaching liquid to 1 cup and pour over the reserved pears. Cool mixture completely and refrigerate. Pears can be prepared two to three days before serving.

BISCUITS:

Place the flour, cocoa, salt, sugar, baking powder and chocolate chips in a large mixing bowl. Blend with a fork. Slowly add the heavy cream, continuing to stir with a fork. Blend until mixture is dampened. Turn out onto a floured surface and with help of a pastry scraper, pat the mixture into a disc 3/4-inch thick. Cut biscuits with a 2 1/2-inch round cutter and place on a well-oiled cookie sheet. Brush tops of biscuits with the melted butter. Place in a preheated 450 degree oven and bake for 15 to 18 minutes until done. Be careful not to scorch; the chocolate burns easily.

Remove to a cooling rack to cool briefly before assembling.

TO ASSEMBLE:

While the biscuits are baking, whip the cream with the poaching liquid until it softly holds its shape. Set aside.

Cut the poached pear pieces in half and set on a plate. When the biscuits have cooled slightly, split them in half. Fan five pear slices on the bottom piece of a biscuit in an attractive pattern. Place a small dollop of whipped cream on top and then place a spoonful or two of poaching liquid over each plate of pears. Place the top half of the biscuit over the pears and place another two spoonfuls of whipped cream on each serving. Serve immediately.

Makes 6 servings.

K. T.

---

4 6-ounce Bartlett pears, peeled and quartered
3 cups water
3/4 cup *real* maple syrup
Juice of 1/2 lemon
....

BISCUITS
1 2/3 cup cake flour
1/2 cup cocoa
1 teaspoon salt
1 tablespoon sugar
1 tablespoon baking powder
1/3 cup miniature chocolate chips
1 cup heavy cream
2 tablespoons melted, unsalted butter
....

GARNISH
1/2 cup heavy cream
2 tablespoons reduced poaching liquid

THE GREAT GRILLED CHEESE

*T*he great grilled cheese! The gorgeous, gooey, golden grilled cheese—an American classic. Who amongst us has not studied a menu only to find the most comforting (and likely the safest) item on it is a simple piece of cheese between two slices of white bread. Said sandwich is treated to heat and comes forth oozing its golden center on our plate. Very frequently this all-American item comes in tandem with a bowl of hot soup. Tomato, in particular, holds a natural affinity.

Well, we love to take classics and provide a current flair. To do so, we are going to provide four delicious combinations of grilled cheese and great soup. Save any one of these for a night when the world has been a bit unkind. You'll feel lots better.

Grandpa Irving's Lentil and Barley Soup...The High-End Grilled Cheese Sandwich
•
Chicken Hominy Soup...Grilled Emmenthaler on Cornmeal-Onion Bread
•
The Crystal's Manhattan Clam Chowder...Open-Faced Kasseri Grills
•
Cantaloupe and Peach Champagne Soup...Feta Grills on Cardamom Raisin Bread

Diane does not stray far from the classic mode with her combination of Lentil and Barley Soup from her grandfather's kitchen and High-End Grilled Cheese on rye bread.

Dan also stays pretty close to home when he assembles a fine sandwich using Grilled Emmenthaler on Cornmeal-Onion Bread. He serves this sandwich with a fantastic Chicken Hominy Soup. Here, that old, classic tomato soup pokes up its head in a new and wonderful format.

Georgia and I move to more far-flung regions for our combinations. She, as is often the case, gets her inspiration from Greece and puts together an Open-faced Grilled Kasseri Sandwich using Kasseri cheese, oregano, and olive oil. Tomato touches her soup again in a fine version of Manhattan Clam Chowder.

I really swerve from the classic mode with a grilled cheese and soup pairing that would be wonderful for a brunch or summer lunch. I have always loved chilled soups, and this soup, which uses fresh, ripe peaches, and cantaloupe, and a sparkling wine, is just wonderful near the end of summer. I suggest serving the soup with Feta Grills on Cardamom Raisin Bread. A touch of marinated cucumber adds some green and crunch to an unusual but delicious sandwich.

Beverages with any of these soup and sandwich combinations should be simple and light. Diane's and Dan's recipes would best be paired with a light red wine (Beaujolais-Villages would be great) or beer. Georgia's and mine are nicely complemented by a white wine. A crisp Spanish Rioja or Italian Soave would be excellent with Georgia's Kasseri sandwich. I would recommend serving my soup and sandwich combination with the same Gewürztraminer used in the soup.

Kathleen Taggart

GRANDPA IRVING'S LENTIL AND BARLEY SOUP

My grandfather used to make a heartwarming, down-home lentil and barley soup. I enjoyed it as a child, but now, as a critical cook, I have taken the same recipe and given it a more robust finish! My husband, who hails from Kansas City, believes that a little Bryant's Barbecue Sauce couldn't hurt a recipe, and in this instance he was right on the mark. If you don't happen to have a bottle of Bryant's on the pantry shelf (we always do), a full-bodied, vinegar-style barbecue sauce can be substituted.

Place the first seven ingredients in a 10 to 12 quart soup pot. Bring to a boil over high heat, skim the surface of the soup, then partially cover and let simmer slowly for two hours.

To finish the soup, add 2 to 3 cups of hot water to thin the soup as desired. Add the rest of the ingredients and taste. Correct the seasonings, if necessary, and serve. This soup freezes beautifully, hence the large quantity. If you would rather make a smaller batch, divide the recipe in half.

Makes 4 quarts.

1/3 cup fine barley (washed and drained)
1 cup lentils (washed and drained)
2 stalks celery, diced
3 onions, diced
4 carrots, peeled and diced
1 pound sirloin tip, trimmed and diced
4 quarts cold water
· · · · · · · · · · · · · · · · ·
2-3 cups water
2/3 cup barbecue sauce
1/3 cup Madeira wine
2 tablespoons sugar
1 1/2 tablespoons coarse salt
Freshly ground black pepper, to taste
1/4 teaspoon freshly ground nutmeg

THE HIGH-END GRILLED CHEESE SANDWICH

Most people think of a grilled cheese sandwich as two pieces of presliced American cheese grilled on two slices of white bread. My version of grilled cheese uses aged, extra sharp cheddar cheese; wonderful pumpernickel rye bread; Vidalia or Walla Walla sweet onions; and a hint of dijon mustard. This is why I call it high-end grilled cheese!

Arrange the slices of bread in pairs, ready for sandwich-making. Thinly spread the dijon mustard on 6 slices of the bread. Place a slice of cheese on top, then a slice of onion. Place another slice of bread on top and butter completely.

Heat a griddle until moderately hot but not smoking. Place the buttered-side of the sandwiches down and grill until nicely browned. Before turning, spread butter on the side facing up. Turn the sandwiches over and grill until nicely browned. Cut in half or quarters and serve immediately.

Makes 6 sandwiches.

12 slices good-quality pumpernickel rye bread
Dijon mustard
3/4 pound aged, extra sharp cheddar cheese
(I use Tillamook Special Reserve),
thickly sliced
6 thin slices Vidalia or Walla Walla sweet
onion
· · · · · · · · · · · · · · · · ·
Unsalted butter, softened

CHICKEN HOMINY SOUP

1 10-ounce can chicken broth
1 1/4 cup water
1 15-ounce can (white or yellow) hominy, drained, liquid reserved
1 whole or two half chicken breasts, skinned and boned
3 tablespoons olive oil
1/2 cup diced onion
1 1/2-inch piece carrot, diced
2 cloves garlic, thinly sliced
1/4 teaspoon cayenne
1 teaspoon paprika
1 cup heavy cream
Coarse salt and freshly ground black pepper, to taste
1 medium tomato, peeled, seeded and diced
1/4 cup chopped fresh cilantro

Place the chicken broth, water, and hominy liquid in a medium saucepan. Add the chicken breast(s) and bring the liquid to a simmer. Cook the chicken *just* until it is barely cooked, about 155 degrees on an instant read thermometer. Remove the meat from the liquid and set it aside to cool. Turn off the heat under the poaching liquid.

*I*n a 5-quart saucepan, heat the olive oil, then add the onion, carrot, and garlic and sauté until the vegetables are soft but not browned. Add the chicken poaching liquids, cayenne, and paprika. Bring the soup to a simmer. In a food processor or blender, puree the hominy, using some of the soup liquid, then add the puree to the soup. Simmer about 10 minutes. Add the cream, and taste the soup. Then add salt and freshly ground black pepper, to taste.

*C*ut the chicken into pieces about 1-inch long and 1/4-inch wide. Add the chicken, tomato, and cilantro to the soup just before serving.

Serves 6 to 8.

GRILLED EMMENTHALER ON CORNMEAL-ONION BREAD

1 loaf Cornmeal-Onion Bread
Dijon mustard
3 slices Swiss Emmenthaler per sandwich
4-6 tablespoons unsalted butter, melted

A recipe for a grilled cheese sandwich? Well, like my wife—and other knowledgeable types—I have strong opinions about just how such a humble morsel should be dealt with! The cornmeal-onion bread offered herein is worlds apart from the cottony "balloon bread" usually associated with grilled cheese sandwiches! And, like Kathleen, I believe that dijon mustard was put on this earth in part to be married with good cheese between two slices of quality bread. Some will insist that a fine, hoppy Pilsner-style beer evolved out of the Cosmic Soup just to accompany such a sandwich. I'm not here to sway you one way or the other, but before you make up your mind, you might want to try a glass of, say, Czechoslovakia's Pilsner Urquell. A crisp, cold, kosher dill pickle on the side is optional. If you have access to the cold-pack jars filled with really crisp, snappy cucumbers perfumed with real garlic and dill, those are mandatory!

*F*or each sandwich cut two 1/2-inch thick slices of the cornmeal-onion bread. Spread a little of your favorite dijon mustard on each slice, and place two or three slices of Swiss Emmenthaler cheese between the mustard-coated bread. Brush the outsides of the sandwich with melted butter and grill in a hot pan or griddle until the bread is golden and the cheese is hot.

Makes 6-8 sandwiches.

CORNMEAL-ONION BREAD

This makes one large loaf. The bread is pleasantly crunchy with a nice onion flavor in the background!

Stir the yeast and sugar into the warm water and allow to sit until foamy, about 5 minutes. Stir in the egg and olive oil.

In a 6-cup capacity food processor fitted with the metal blade, process the flour, cornmeal, salt, and onion until the onion is cut into very small pieces, probably about 10 to 15 seconds. Remove the metal blade and fit the machine with the dough blade if so equipped.

Stir the liquids well and, with the machine running, slowly pour them into the workbowl. The dough should form a ball and, after a few seconds, begin to rotate inside the machine. Allow the dough to revolve (knead) in the machine for 1 minute. Add a tablespoon or more of flour to control the stickiness if necessary.

Remove the dough from the machine and place it in a gallon-size plastic bag. Squeeze out all the air from the bag and place a wire twist at the *top* of the bag so that the dough has room to expand. Allow the dough to rest and rise in a warm place until it is double its original size.

Remove the dough from the bag and shape into a loaf which will fit into a well-greased 9x5 loaf pan. Cover the loaf with greased plastic wrap and allow it to rise until the top of the dough is about one inch above the sides of the pan. Carefully remove the plastic wrap. Brush the top of the loaf very gently with beaten egg if you like, for a shiny, brown look.

Bake in a preheated 375 degree oven for about 35 to 40 minutes, until an instant read thermometer registers 200 degrees. Cool on a rack after removing from the pan.

Makes 1 loaf.

1 cup warm water, not over 115 degrees
1 tablespoon or 1 package active dry yeast
1 teaspoon sugar
1 large egg
3 tablespoons olive oil
About 2 3/4 cups all-purpose, unbleached flour
1 cup yellow or white cornmeal
1 teaspoon coarse salt
About 3 ounces onion, cut in several small pieces
....
1 egg

2 dozen live, hard-shell clams, *or*
2 6 1/2-ounce cans chopped clams with liquid

· · · · · · · · · · · · · · · · · ·

1/4 cup olive oil

1 large clove garlic, minced

1 large onion, chopped

2 stalks celery with leaves, chopped

3 carrots, peeled and thinly sliced

1 28-ounce can peeled tomatoes, chopped, with liquid

1/2 cup parsley, minced

1 teaspoon thyme, or 1 tablespoon fresh thyme

1 bay leaf

2 medium boiling potatoes, cut into 1/2-inch cubes

Coarse salt and freshly ground black pepper, to taste

THE CRYSTAL'S MANHATTAN CLAM CHOWDER

The Crystal was the name of my family's restaurant in southeastern Pennsylvania. My favorite memory of Friday night supper was a large bowl of this tomato-based chowder with a slice of warm Jewish rye bread with caraway seeds and butter on it! Because Saturday was the Sabbath, the bakery made the week-end breads on Friday, delivering them warm in the afternoon. Since it was unsliced, you could cut your own slice as thick as you wanted!!!

Clean the clam shells well and place in a large pot, covering with water. Steam until they open. Remove the clams from their shells and chop fine. Strain the broth and reserve.

Clean the large pot you steamed the clams in and dry well. Heat the oil and add the garlic, onion, celery, and carrots. Sauté over medium heat until the vegetables are soft and the onions are transparent. Add the tomatoes and clam liquid, parsley, thyme, and bay leaf. Cover and simmer for about an hour, adding a little water if the soup becomes too thick. The soup shouldn't be thin, so don't add much.

Add the potatoes and chopped clams and simmer for another 15 minutes or until the potatoes are cooked. Add the salt and pepper, to taste. To give the soup a little "bite," I use more than an ordinary amount of black pepper, usually a full teaspoon to start.

Remove the bay leaf and let the soup stand for about 15 minutes off the heat before you serve it. The "traditional" way to serve it is with oyster crackers on top.

Serves 6 to 8.

OPEN-FACED KASSERI GRILLS

This sandwich is grilled open-faced under the broiler. I recommend a rye bread with caraway seeds, purchased unsliced so you can slice it as thick or as thin as you like. Presliced rye breads are often not tasty—the best come from a bakery not the grocery store !! Kasseri cheese can be found in two versions—domestic or imported. They are very different. You might try both and see which one you like best. Domestic Kasseri can be found in the deli section of most grocery stores. It tastes a lot like romano cheese—sharp and firm-textured. Imported Kasseri is softer and mellower. It can be found in Greek grocery stores or specialty food stores. I prefer the imported variety for this sandwich.

Toast the bread until somewhat dried out and firm but not actually toasted. Brush some of the olive oil on each slice. Sprinkle with two tablespoons of the oregano. Cover the bread with cheese.

Place on a baking pan in a 400 degree oven for about 10 minutes or until the cheese is soft. Turn on the broiler and watch carefully until the cheese is completely melted. Don't let it burn. When melted, sprinkle the remaining tablespoon of oregano on top.

Serve immediately.

Serves 6.

6 thick slices rye bread
1 tablespoon extra-virgin olive oil
3 tablespoons chopped fresh oregano
  or 3 teaspoons dried
8 ounces Kasseri cheese, cut into 6 slices

1/2 medium cantaloupe, peeled and seeded

3 medium peaches, peeled and pitted

1/2 cup sugar

1/2 cup Gewürztraminer wine (lightly sweet)

1 cup dry champagne or sparkling wine

3 tablespoons pistachios, chopped

CANTALOUPE AND PEACH CHAMPAGNE SOUP

This is a great soup for brunch, a first course, or even a light dessert. It can be made in advance up to the addition of the champagne, which should be added right before serving.

Place the peeled cantaloupe and peaches in the workbowl of a food processor fitted with the metal blade. Add the sugar and puree until no pieces of fruit remain and it is smooth. Add the Gewürztraminer wine and blend quickly. Remove soup to a bowl and place in the refrigerator to chill. Just before serving, blend in the champagne with a whisk and ladle into serving bowls. Garnish with chopped pistachios.

Serves 6.

K. T.

1/2 medium cucumber, peeled and sliced with 2mm slicer of food processor

2 tablespoons seasoned Japanese rice vinegar

12 slices Cardamom Raisin Bread (recipe follows), or good quality raisin bread without cinnamon

Sesame tahini

8 ounces feta cheese

Olive oil

FETA GRILLS ON CARDAMOM RAISIN BREAD

Marinate the sliced cucumber in the seasoned rice vinegar for at least a half hour before assembling the sandwiches.

Spread six slices of the bread with the sesame tahini. Top this with feta cheese sliced as best as possible with a cheese planer. (It will crumble, but just sprinkle crumbs on top.) Top the cheese with slices of the marinated cucumber. Place the second slice of bread on top and brush both sides of the sandwiches with olive oil. Grill the sandwiches on a hot griddle until well-browned on both sides.

Makes 6 sandwiches.

K. T.

CARDAMOM RAISIN BREAD

Simmer the wheat berries in boiling water for 30 to 40 minutes. Pour into a colander and rinse under cold water until cool. Drain well and reserve. Soak the raisins in the liqueur for at least a half hour before using.

When ready to make the bread, place the dry yeast in the warm water for approximately 10 minutes until it becomes foamy. In the meantime, drain the wheat berries and place them along with the flour in the workbowl of a food processor fitted with the metal blade. Turn the machine on and run for about 30 seconds until the berries are partially chopped but some texture remains. Add the salt and cardamom to the workbowl and pulse once or twice to blend. Change to the plastic dough blade. When the yeast mixture is foamy, add to it the oil and honey. With the machine on, slowly pour the liquid mixture through the feed tube until a ball is formed, adding either a bit more flour or water if necessary to get the correct consistency of dough. Allow the dough ball to knead for 60 to 90 seconds. Remove the dough ball from the processor and place in a well-oiled bowl. Cover and allow to rise until doubled in bulk.

Punch down the dough and knead in the soaked raisins by hand. Place the dough in a large, well-oiled bread pan. Cover lightly with oiled plastic wrap and again allow to double in bulk.

Preheat oven to 375 degrees. Bake the bread for approximately 30 minutes or until the internal temperature reaches 180 degrees. Remove from the bread pan and return to the oven for a couple of minutes to crisp the bottom crust. Allow to cool completely.

Makes 1 large (1 1/2-pound) loaf or 2 smaller ones.

K. T.

1/2 cup wheat berries
1/2 cup raisins
2 tablespoons Mandarin Napoleon Liqueur (or other orange liqueur)
1 tablespoon dry yeast
1 cup warm water (105 to 115 degrees)
3 cups all-purpose flour
2 teaspoons coarse salt
2 teaspoons cardamom
1/4 cup vegetable oil
1/4 cup honey

MEMORIES OF INDIA

*T*he memories referred to in this menu's title are of several restaurants in England, Scotland, and the United States, and of many wonderful meals created at home following the recipes of Julie Sahni, Madhur Jaffrey, and Yamuna Devi in their books on Indian cooking.

Pakoras

•

Yogurt-Mint Chutney

•

Velvet Butter Fish

•

Coconut Chutney

•

Indian Rice Pilaf

•

Crisp Fried Okra with Peanuts

•

Raita

•

Toasted Cashew and Banana Ice Cream

Indian cooking is aromatic! The mix of herbs and spices used literally fills the kitchen with enticing smells. Even confirmed steak and potato eaters run the risk of changing their diet. More than 800 million Indians make dried lentils, chick-peas, aromatic rices, chapati flour, fresh vegetables, and fresh and dried seasonings the main ingredients of their diet. And, depending on religious preference, cultural training and geographic location an Indian's diet may include some meat, poultry or fish. However, whether your preference is for vegetarian or not, I promise you that Indian seasonings will addict you!

Much of Indian cooking is spicy; the use of fresh chili is liberal, to put it mildly. We've written recipes which we think will be interesting but not offensive to most people. (I suggest, by the way, that you never say to a waiter in an Indian restaurant—as I once did—that, in spite of his warning about the spiciness of a dish, "It can't be too hot!" It was, and all the accompanying condiments were too! I bravely consumed my meal, but it took three months for my stomach to return to normal.) The beauty of home cooking is that you may do exactly as you please: toss in handfuls of chopped fresh chilies, or use almost none. Indian seasonings will please you either way, we think. If this is your first experience with the flavors of Indian food, it's alright to start smiling now in anticipation. You will on first bite anyway!

Dan Taggart

Fresh vegetables, about 2 cups of each
2 cups chick-pea flour (also called garbanzo flour), found in health food stores
1 teaspoon coarse salt
2 teaspoons ground cumin
1 tablespoon vegetable or peanut oil
1 1/2 to 2 cups cold water
About 4 cups of oil for frying

PAKORAS

These fried vegetables are delicious. Any vegetables can be used, but I like a mix of vegetables of different colors, such as cauliflower, broccoli, yams, mushrooms, eggplant, and so on. Some of the vegetables may need to be dredged in flour before dipping in the batter because they won't absorb enough batter otherwise. This holds true for the yams, mushrooms, and eggplant.

After washing the vegetables, cut the cauliflower and broccoli into flowerets. The yams should be cut into "french fry" size pieces about 1/2 inch wide. Mushrooms should be left whole. The eggplant should be cut into round slices and then cut in half or quarters depending on the size. You can also use zucchini. The goal is to have a variety of colors and shapes to make an attractive plate.

In the workbowl of a food processor fitted with the metal blade, place all the dry ingredients and oil and process for about 10 seconds. Add the cold water and process until smooth. Put the batter in a bowl, cover, and let "rest" in a warm place for about 15 to 20 minutes.

Heat the oil in a frying pan to 375 degrees. Dip the vegetable pieces into the batter and fry until golden brown, turning to cook evenly. Drain the cooked pieces on paper towels.

Serve with Yogurt-Mint Chutney.

Makes 8 appetizer servings.

3 large cloves garlic
1 1-inch piece of ginger, peeled
2 teaspoons garam masala
3 green onions
1 cup fresh mint leaves
1/2 cup fresh cilantro leaves
1/2 of a hot red or jalapeño chili
1/2 mild green chili
1/3 cup plain yogurt

YOGURT-MINT CHUTNEY

Put all the ingredients except the yogurt in blender and purée. Remove from the blender and stir in the yogurt.

Chill until serving time.

VELVET BUTTER FISH

I am indebted to Julie Sahni for this recipe's inspiration. Dan and I have used her two volumes on Indian cooking for a couple of years and have loved the results. This is an adaptation of a recipe called Velvet Butter Chicken which uses leftover Tandoori chicken. I thought it would work very well with fish. I toned down the spices a bit so as not to overwhelm the fish and I think the results are delicious.

Chop the garlic and ginger for the marinade. Add all the other ingredients: the roasted cumin, ground cardamom, red pepper, paprika, and yogurt. Blend in a blender or food chopper. Pour marinade over the fish. Rub into both sides and allow the fish to sit in the marinade for 1/2 hour. In the meantime, heat the grill. When ready to grill, scrape the marinade off the fish, reserving the marinade. Pat the fish dry, and then rub both sides of the fish with vegetable oil. Grill the fish over a hot fire until it reaches an internal temperature of 110 degrees. (The fish will not be fully cooked, but you will be reheating it, and you definitely do not want it overcooked!) Remove the fish from the grill. Allow to cool and then cut into 1/2-inch size chunks. Proceed to make the sauce while the fish is cooling.

Chop the jalapeño chilies and the ginger root in a blender or food processor. Add the canned tomatoes and the leftover marinade and blend until pureed. In a 3-quart sauté pan, melt the butter over medium heat. Add the ground cumin and the paprika and stir for about 2 minutes until it smells "toasty." Add the tomato mixture and bring to a simmer. Allow the tomato mixture to simmer until it thickens and the volume is reduced by half. This will probably take 20 minutes to a half an hour. Add the heavy cream and the salt. Heat thoroughly. Just before serving add the cut up swordfish, the ground roasted cumin, and the garam masala. Cover and heat gently for about five minutes. Sprinkle the chopped fresh coriander over the dish and serve immediately.

Serves 8.

K.T.

1 large garlic clove
1 teaspoon freshly minced ginger
1/2 teaspoon roasted cumin seed, ground
1/4 teaspoon ground cardamom
Pinch dried red pepper flakes
1 teaspoon paprika
1/4 cup plain yogurt

· · · · · · · · · · · · · · · · · · · ·

1 3/4 pounds fresh swordfish or other firm-fleshed fish

· · · · · · · · · · · · · · · · · · · ·

2 green jalapeño chilies, seeded
1 tablespoon freshly minced ginger root
1 28-ounce can whole tomatoes
2 tablespoons butter
2 teaspoons ground cumin
1 teaspoon paprika
1 teaspoon salt
1 cup heavy cream
1 1/2 teaspoons roasted cumin, ground
1 teaspoon garam masala
1/4 cup fresh chopped coriander

COCONUT CHUTNEY

1 coconut, shelled, peeled and shredded*

3 tablespoons vegetable oil or clarified butter

1 teaspoon black or brown mustard seeds

1/2 teaspoon asafetida powder

2 scallions, cut in 1-inch pieces

1 green jalapeño chili, seeded

1 packed cup fresh cilantro

1 packed cup fresh parsley

3/4 cup sesame seeds, toasted

1 rounded teaspoon tamarind paste dissolved in 1/3 cup boiling water

1 1/2 cups plain yogurt, approximately

1 teaspoon coarse salt

1 teaspoon sugar

2 teaspoons dark-colored sesame oil

Chutneys are relishes served with Indian meals. They are made from a great variety of foods and can be sweet and sour, hot and spicy, chunky and jam-like, or thin and almost watery. The bottled mango-based concoctions on the supermarket shelf are but one type. Here is a completely different preparation. You'll need to visit an Indian or Pakistani market, most likely, to find a couple of the ingredients. If that's impractical, don't panic! American chunky-style cranberry sauce wouldn't be a bad accompaniment to this meal! Or make Diane's Cranberry Chutney from ENTERTAINING PEOPLE.

In a small, heavy frypan, heat the oil or butter over medium high heat. Add the mustard seed and cover the pan with a spatter shield or loosely-placed lid. When most of the seeds have popped, remove the pan from the heat. Cool for a minute or two and then stir in the asafetida powder. Set aside.

In the workbowl of a food processor fitted with the metal blade, mince the scallions and jalapeño. Add the cilantro and parsley and thoroughly mince them as well. Add the shredded coconut, sesame seeds, tamarind/water mixture, yogurt, salt, sugar, sesame oil, and the mustard/asafetida mixture. Run the machine until all the ingredients are thoroughly mixed and the chutney is a uniformly grainy texture. The chutney should be neither watery nor the thickness of mashed potatoes; adjust the texture by adding a bit more yogurt if necessary. Serve in a small bowl to be passed at the table.

* In order to shell fresh coconut without resorting to a sledgehammer, insert a sharp skewer or awl through at least two of the "eyes" and shake out the liquid. Place the nut on a baking sheet in a 400 degree oven until the shell cracks, approximately 15 to 20 minutes. When the nut has cooled a bit, smack the shell with a meat pounder or other heavy object to split the nut open. Pry the meat out and remove the brown skin with a vegetable peeler.

INDIAN RICE PILAF

If you've never been lucky enough to have eaten Basmati, an especially aromatic rice grown in areas of India and Pakistan, then by all means find an Indian specialty store or an oriental food market where it is sold. You may never eat any other rice again. This pilaf is a beautiful light yellow color because of the turmeric. The recipe calls for a spice mixture called garam masala. Look for it at Middle Eastern or Indian food stores or make your own. See page 106 in ENTERTAINING PEOPLE for the recipe. Since we're using a fresh coconut in the chutney, the coconut milk can be used in the pilaf. Otherwise use all water.

Rinse the rice in several changes of cold water, swishing and stirring to separate any loose husks or other impurities. Drain. Place the rice in a bowl and cover with the 4 cups of liquid. Let stand for about 30 minutes. Drain, but reserve the soaking liquid. It will be used in the cooking. If using long grain rice, omit the soaking procedure.

Heat a 3 1/2 to 5-quart sauté pan. Add the oils. Toss in the minced ginger and scallion and stir over medium heat for a minute or two. Add the turmeric and 1 teaspoon of the garam masala and cook for another minute. Add the drained rice and cook, stirring the grains, for 3 or 4 minutes. Add the reserved soaking liquid and salt and pepper and stir well. Bring the mixture to a boil, reduce to a simmer, cover and cook over very low heat for 15 minutes without disturbing. Turn off the heat and allow the pilaf to sit undisturbed for another 10 to 15 minutes.

Just before serving stir in the remaining teaspoon of garam masala and the sliced scallion tops.

Note: Leftover pilaf makes a great rewarmed main dish when combined with bits of fish, chicken, sausage, or other meats. Or toss cold leftover pilaf with a full-flavored vinaigrette or quality mayonnaise to make a memorable rice salad!

Serves 6 to 8.

---

2 cups Basmati or long grain rice
Milk of 1 coconut plus water to equal 4 cups
1 tablespoon dark-colored sesame oil
1 tablespoon coconut oil, or substitute vegetable oil
1 tablespoon minced fresh unpeeled ginger
White portion of 6 scallions, minced
1 teaspoon ground turmeric
2 teaspoons garam masala
1 teaspoon salt
Freshly ground black pepper
Green part of 6 scallions, thinly sliced

2 tablespoons oil
2 quarter-sized slices ginger root, minced
1 clove garlic, cut in half
3/4 pound fresh okra, stem-end removed,
sliced into 1/4-inch rounds
3/4 teaspoon ground cumin
1/8 teaspoon cayenne
3/4 teaspoon coarse salt
3/4 teaspoon sugar
1/3 cup dry roasted peanuts
1 large scallion, diced (green included)

1/2 pound cucumber, peeled, seeds removed
and cut into 1/4-inch cubes
1 cup chopped fresh cilantro leaves
3 cups plain yogurt

CRISP FRIED OKRA WITH PEANUTS

An Indian mathematician named V. Srinivas taught me how to make this dish. He is a fine scholar and a wonderful cook who now resides in Bombay. He told me that the key to making this dish was to make sure the okra is crisp. I believe I have faithfully duplicated his technique.

In a 10 to 12-inch heavy bottomed sauté pan, heat the oil over medium high heat. Add the ginger and garlic and sauté about one minute. Add the okra and cook, stirring frequently, until lightly browned. The bright green color should still remain. This step usually takes about 10 minutes. Turn the heat to medium if the okra begins to get too dark.

Once the okra is crisp, add the spices and peanuts. Cook, stirring frequently for about 3 minutes more. Add the scallion, toss to combine, then serve immediately.

Serves 8.

DM

RAITA

In a medium-sized mixing bowl, combine the cucumber, cilantro, and yogurt. Stir thoroughly to combine, then refrigerate until ready to serve.

Serve in individual small bowls to accompany the entree.

Serves 8.

DM

TOASTED CASHEW AND BANANA ICE CREAM

Heat the milk, cream, sugar, and salt in a saucepan until the sugar dissolves. Pureé the bananas in a blender or food processor. Add the sour cream, the Mandarine Napoleon liqueur, and the bananas to the cream mixture. Blend well. Chill for several hours or preferably overnight. Freeze in an ice cream maker according to manufacturer's directions. When the ice cream is nearly set, add the cashew bits and white chocolate chips. Finish freezing until firm.

Makes 2 quarts.

K. T.

1 cup milk
2 cups heavy cream
1 cup sugar
Pinch salt
3 large, very ripe bananas (about 2 cups puréed)
1/2 cup sour cream
1 tablespoon Mandarine Napoleon liqueur
1 cup toasted cashew bits
1/2 cup white chocolate chips

INDULGENCE

Porto Pudim Flan

•

Baklava

•

Berry Banana Trifle

•

Mexican Chocolate Cheesecake

•

The Negus Revisited

•

Raisin and Pecan Filled Triple Chocolate Balls

•

Cinnamon Ice Cream

*I*ndulgence! Now here is a word that fuels the imagination. It is a luxurious word. It invokes images of special times past, present, and future. When we speak of indulgence in relation to food, we are referring to foods we rarely eat. Nowadays desserts are often first on the list of forbidden foods. Our low-calorie, low-cholesterol world practically makes dessert taboo. With all this said, there are times we want to say, who cares—life is here to enjoy. So, to help you in this pursuit, we have planned an indulgent, devilishly decadent dessert buffet for you to share with your friends.

When you are going to indulge your fancy and fantasies in food, do so only with the best. Don't waste your precious calories on mediocre desserts; make sure they are magnificent, like the desserts presented here. Each of these desserts can stand on its own wonderfully after a fine meal, and together, watch out. Just run, swim, or jog a little more aggressively tomorrow.

No dessert assortment would be complete without a few creations that involve glorious chocolate. Three of our seven desserts are indebted to the cocoa plant. Diane offers a beautiful three layer, liqueur-soaked chocolate genoise with a sinfully rich buttercream frosting and filling. Since Diane's "melt-in-your-mouth" cheesecake was such a hit in our first book, she has reworked it here into a Mexican Chocolate Cheesecake. My small claim to chocolate fame is with Raisin and Pecan-Filled Triple Chocolate Balls. These are half-cookie, half-confection with chocolate in the pastry, the filling, and the glaze.

With no shyness or hesitation, Georgia claims that she makes the world's best Baklava. We do not argue and neither will you when you try this Greek classic.

Georgia and I satisfy the tastes of the custard lovers among us — she with a delicious Berry Banana Trifle and I with an updated version of a Portuguese classic, Porto Pudim Flan (or Port Wine Custard).

Absolutely no dessert assortment could be complete without a homemade ice cream. Dan produces a fantastically tasty Cinnamon Ice Cream.

What would be good to drink with such an assortment of sweets? I would choose as good a quality sparkling wine as you can afford. It is always festive and a bit indulgent. A lovely Port would also be appropriate — Ruby, Tawny or a "late-bottled" vintage.

Bring out your best serving pieces (silver will do well here) and fill the house with elegant flowers. This is not an event that happens every night!

Kathleen Taggart

PORTO PUDIM FLAN (PORT WINE CUSTARD)

This is my version of a famous Portuguese dessert that uses Port wine to flavor a luscious baked custard. Try to find a nice Tawny, Ruby, or "late-vintage" Port wine. The fine flavor of any of these will enhance the finished product.

Preheat oven to 350 degrees. In a small 1-quart saucepan, heat the milk and cream until bubbles appear around the edge. In the meantime, take a larger saucepan (at least 2 quarts) and melt the sugar over moderate heat, stirring occasionally, until it is golden brown. Pour the heated milk/cream mixture into the caramel in a slow, steady stream, stirring constantly and being careful not to let it boil over. Continue to stir until all the caramel has dissolved.

Beat the egg yolks manually or with an electric beater until they are well blended. Slowly pour in the cream mixture, stirring constantly with a spoon or whisk. Add the Port wine. Strain the custard into baking cups - 4-ounce size for a standard dessert, or 2 to 3-ounce size for a dessert buffet. Place the cups in a large, shallow baking pan. Pour enough boiling water into the pan to come halfway up the sides of the cups. Bake 40 to 45 minutes until a knife inserted in the custard comes out clean. Cool thoroughly and then refrigerate for several hours before serving.

Makes 8 4-ounce servings.

K. T.

1 1/2 cups milk
1 1/2 cups heavy cream
2/3 cup granulated sugar
6 large egg yolks
2 tablespoons good-quality Port wine

SYRUP

3 cups sugar

Half a cinnamon stick

2 1/2 cups water

5 whole cloves

Juice of 1/2 lemon

Peel of one lemon

2 tablespoons honey

. . . .

3 cups finely chopped or ground nuts (I use 2 cups walnuts and 1 cup almonds)

1 teaspoon ground cinnamon

1/2 teaspoon ground nutmeg

3/4 pound unsalted butter, melted

2 pounds filo

Whole cloves

BAKLAVA

Combine all of the syrup ingredients, except the honey, and bring to a boil. Simmer for 15 minutes, adding the honey for the last 5 minutes. Strain and cool to room temperature. Preheat oven to 350 degrees. Mix the nuts, cinnamon, and nutmeg and set aside. Melt the butter and clarify.

Set a 9x13 metal* pan over the filo sheets and trim the sheets to pan size. The finished baklava has a nicer appearance when there isn't excess dough on the ends, so trimming carefully is important.

Layer 10 sheets of filo in the pan, buttering between each layer. Scatter about 1/4 cup of the nut mixture over the last layer, distributing the nuts evenly.

Continue layering, buttering each sheet and sprinkling a 1/4-cup of the nut mixture over every other layer. Reserve 12 sheets of filo for the top layers.

Layer the last 12 sheets of filo, buttering each sheet, but do not use any of the nut filling. Butter the top layer very well.

With a sharp knife, cut the baklava into 5 rows lengthwise. Make diamond shapes by cutting diagonally across the rows. Place a whole clove in the center of each piece.

Bake at 350 degrees for 30 minutes, then lower the heat to 300 degrees and bake for an hour. If the baklava begins to brown too quickly, lower the heat to 275 degrees. One of the secrets of good baklava is long, slow baking. This way, it bakes all the way through without getting too brown. It should take up to 2 hours total for the baklava to finish baking and be nicely browned. Check a center piece to make sure the filo dough is baked all the way through.

Remove and cool 15 minutes on a cooling rack. Slowly pour *room temperature* syrup over the baklava, and allow to stand until completely cooled. You will use about 2 1/2 cups syrup for this size pan. Cut through the pieces again when the baklava is cool. It is traditional to serve the baklava in paper muffin cups.

Makes approximately 36 pieces.

* The baklava bakes more evenly and browns nicer in a metal pan, however, if all you have is a glass baking dish, it will work as well.

BERRY BANANA TRIFLE

The base of this trifle is a cake. You can use any kind you like—pound cake, angel food, genoise—and it can be homemade or purchased. It doesn't need to be a very fancy, rich cake because all the other ingredients make it rich and fancy. I like to use fresh berries, but you can use frozen ones when fresh are not available. Diane made this trifle for her son's birthday party. She plumped the raisins in warm water, then drained them. And she substituted a chocolate sauce, which she thinned slightly with water, for the Kahlua. It made a wonderful non-alcoholic variation.

Soak the currants in the Kahlua for one hour. Mix the sugar with the fresh strawberries, and set aside. If you are using the frozen berries, make sure they are completely thawed.

Make the creme anglaise and cool to room temperature.

Arrange half of the cake cubes in the bottom of a glass bowl. A trifle dish makes a lovely presentation, but any glass bowl shows this dessert to advantage. Drain the currants, reserving the Kahlua. Pour half of the Kahlua over the cake pieces. Spread half the berries and their juice over the cake. Put the slices of one banana on top of this. Spread one cup of the creme anglaise over the bananas and sprinkle half of the currants on top. Repeat with the remaining cake, Kahlua, berries and juice, bananas, creme anglaise, and currants. Cover tightly with plastic wrap and refrigerate until serving time.

Whip the cream with the powdered sugar and spread on top of the trifle. Garnish with the almonds and some whole fresh berries.

Serves 10 to 12.

CREME ANGLAISE

Mix the cornstarch and sugar in a bowl. Heat the milk over medium heat until a skin forms on top and the milk begins to rise in the pot. Remove from the heat and pour half of it into the cornstarch mixture, whisking to mix. Stir the egg yolks with a fork to blend and add to the mixture in the bowl, mixing well. Put the remaining milk back on the stove and add the other mixture to it. Cook over medium heat until it thickens, about 2 minutes. Remove from the heat and add the vanilla. Allow the mixture to cool slightly. Beat the egg whites until stiff but not dry. Carefully fold into the cooled custard. Place a piece of plastic wrap directly on top of the custard so a skin won't form on top and refrigerate until cold.

1/4 cup dried currants
1 cup Kahlua, or other liqueur
1/4 cup sugar
2 cups sliced fresh strawberries or,
2 10-ounce packages frozen strawberries with juice (omit sugar)
2 cups Creme Anglaise (recipe follows)
8 cups of 1-inch cake cubes, such as 1 10-ounce frozen pound cake
2 bananas, sliced
1 cup heavy cream, whipped
2 tablespoons powdered sugar
1/4 cup toasted, slivered almonds
Additional whole berries, for garnish

....

CREME ANGLAISE
1/4 cup cornstarch
1/2 cup sugar
2 cups milk
2 eggs, separated
1 teaspoon vanilla

CRUST

1 (8 1/2)-ounce box chocolate wafers*
1 1/2 tablespoons sugar
Pinch coarse salt
2 teaspoons ground cinnamon
5 tablespoons butter, melted

. . . .

FILLING

8 ounces semisweet chocolate
2 tablespoons whipping cream
1 1/2 pounds cream cheese, room temperature
1 cup sugar
2 large eggs, room temperature
1 1/2 teaspoons vanilla
1 tablespoon ground cinnamon
1/3 cup double strength, cooled espresso
1 cup sour cream

. . . .

GARNISH

2 tablespoons powdered sugar
2 tablespoons Dutch-processed cocoa

. . . .

9-inch springform or 2-piece cheesecake pan

MEXICAN CHOCOLATE CHEESECAKE

The inspiration for this cheesecake came from eating some superb Mexican chocolate ice cream which combines chocolate and cinnamon. Having already made several mocha cheesecake recipes, I decided to experiment by adding cinnamon to both the crust and filling. I was delighted with the results...and think you will be, too.

Preheat the oven to 350 degrees. In the workbowl of a food processor, process *3/4* of the package (about 6-ounces) of chocolate wafers until finely ground. (Save the remainder for another use. I eat them!) Add the sugar, salt, and cinnamon and process to combine. Mound the wafer crumbs in the middle of the pan. Make a well in the center and pour in the butter. Using your fingers, thoroughly combine the butter and crumbs. Press the crust evenly around the bottom and about 1/3 of the way up the sides of the pan. (I use a 1-cup stainless measuring cup to do this since it helps prevent the corners from being thicker than the sides.)

Bake the crust 8 to 10 minutes. Remove to a cooling rack and use the measuring cup again to press the crust flat. Let cool while you are making the filling.

Melt the chocolate and cream together, then let cool.

Clean the workbowl of the food processor. Process the cream cheese and the sugar until smooth and thoroughly combined. Add the eggs, vanilla, and cinnamon to the workbowl and process until incorporated. Add the melted chocolate mixture and process to combine. Then add the cooled espresso and the sour cream and pulse to combine. Make sure the filling is lump-free or else you will have lumps in the finished cheesecake.

Gently pour the filling into the pan. The filling may come up slightly higher than the crust. This is not a problem. Place the pan in the preheated oven and bake for 45 to 50 minutes or until the sides are slightly puffed. The center third of the cake will still be very soft and unset when you gently shake the pan. Turn off the oven and leave the cheesecake in the oven, undisturbed, for 20 minutes. Then remove it and cool it on a rack before refrigerating. Leave the cheesecake in the pan during refrigeration. If cracks appear on the surface, you baked it a little too long. This will not affect the flavor and you can hide the evidence with the cocoa-powdered sugar mixture or some shaved chocolate or whipped cream.

To garnish the cake, combine the powdered sugar and dutch cocoa and mix thoroughly. Place in a fine mesh sifter and sift evenly over the top of the cake. Remove the sides of the cheesecake pan, slice, and serve.

Makes 1 9-inch cheesecake to serve 10 to 14.

* I use "Famous Chocolate Wafers" by Nabisco.

DM

THE NEGUS REVISITED

This is an adaptation of a recipe that first appeared in SPHERE Magazine (later to be called CUISINE Magazine) in September 1977. The fact that this recipe remains in my "active" file says something for its appeal. I adore this cake. It is chocolate, chocolate, and more chocolate with the wonderful flavorings of hazelnut liqueur and coffee.

Preheat the oven to 325 degrees. Butter and flour a 10-inch springform pan. In a large mixer bowl beat the egg yolks, sugar, and salt until thick and lemon colored, about 5 minutes. Sift the flour and cocoa together; add gradually to the egg yolk mixture. (The batter will be very thick at this stage.) In a separate mixer bowl beat the egg whites until foamy, then add the cream of tartar. Beat until the egg whites form nice peaks but are not dry. With a rubber spatula take one large "glob" of the egg whites and thoroughly incorporate them into the batter. Because the batter is quite thick at this stage, a little care and patience will be required; however, the resulting mixture will be much easier to work with. Then continue to gently fold the remaining egg whites into the batter, in batches.

Spoon the batter into the prepared pan and bake until a toothpick inserted into the center comes out clean. Test the cake after one hour, although it may take as long as one and a half hours, depending on your oven. Cool on a rack for 5 minutes. Remove the springform side. Invert the cake onto another cooling rack, remove the springform bottom. The bottom will now become the top of the finished cake. Cool completely.

To make the syrup, combine the sugar and water in a small saucepan. Stir to dissolve the sugar, then bring to a boil over medium heat. Allow to boil two minutes, then remove from the heat and cool. Stir in the Frangelica and reserve.

To make the buttercream, first melt the two chocolates together and set aside to cool. Beat the egg yolks, powdered sugar, and salt in a large mixer bowl until the sugar is dissolved and the mixture forms ribbons, about 5 minutes. On medium speed beat in the cooled chocolate and coffee. Now add the butter, one tablespoon at a time. Beat well after each addition until smooth and fluffy. Reserve.

To assemble the cake, make a vertical notch in the side of the cake. It should run the entire height of the cake and be about 1/4-inch deep. This cut allows you to realign the cake once you have separated the layers. Now cut the cake into 3 even horizontal layers. I use a very sharp serrated bread knife for this task.

If you have a small spray or pump bottle, put the liqueur/syrup mixture into it and spray each layer with about one third of this mixture. Otherwise brush or sprinkle on the syrup. (I keep a small spray bottle expressly for this use.)

Spread about 2/3 cup of the buttercream between each layer, realigning the cake as you go. Now spread additional buttercream smoothly around the sides of the cake. Place the remaining buttercream in a pastry bag with a 1/4-inch plain tip, and make parallel lines across the top of the cake. (Use a coupler so that you can switch decorating tips at this point.) Now use a decorating tip to make rosettes around the rim of the cake. Place a chocolate-covered coffee bean in the center of each rosette, or allow enough space between the rosettes to place the coffee bean there. If you wish, sprinkle the grated chocolate on the sides of the cake. Refrigerate the cake. Remove from the refrigerator about 30 minutes before serving. (This cake also freezes beautifully.)

Makes one 10-inch cake to serve 10 to 12.

GENOISE
8 extra-large egg yolks
2 cups sugar
1/2 teaspoon coarse salt
1 cup all-purpose flour
2/3 cup Dutch-processed cocoa
12 extra-large egg whites
1 teaspoon cream of tartar
....

SYRUP
1/4 cup sugar
1/2 cup water
3 tablespoons Frangelica (hazelnut liqueur)
....

CHOCOLATE BUTTERCREAM
1 ounce unsweetened chocolate
3 ounces semisweet chocolate
4 extra-large egg yolks
2 cups powdered sugar
1/4 teaspoon coarse salt
2 tablespoons double strength, cooled espresso
3/4 pound unsalted butter, room temperature
....

GARNISH
Chocolate covered coffee beans
1/2 cup finely grated semisweet chocolate

CHOCOLATE PASTRY

1 1/2 cups all-purpose flour
1/2 cup unsweetened cocoa
1/2 cup sugar
Pinch salt
1 1/2 sticks (6 ounces) unsalted butter, chilled
1 egg
1 teaspoon vanilla
1/2 teaspoon orange extract

. . . .

FILLING

2 cups chopped toasted pecans
2/3 cup chopped raisins
1/2 teaspoon orange extract
1 teaspoon unsweetened cocoa powder
1 tablespoon honey
3/4 cup red wine

. . . .

8 ounces good quality semisweet or bittersweet chocolate (Guittard or Callebaut are good choices)
Vegetable oil, a few drops as needed to thin chocolate

RAISIN AND PECAN-FILLED TRIPLE CHOCOLATE BALLS

Frequently the idea for a new recipe and its finished product can be quite divergent, but these yummy chocolate balls turned out just as I had imagined – a tender, fruity, nutty center surrounded by crisp pastry and dipped in fine bittersweet chocolate. They freeze beautifully.

To make the chocolate pastry, place the flour, cocoa, sugar, and salt in the workbowl of a food processor fitted with the metal blade. Pulse once or twice to mix. Cut the butter into tablespoon-size pieces and add to the food processor. Pulse the machine several times until the butter is the size of peas. Mix together the egg, vanilla, and orange extract. With the machine running, pour the egg mixture through the feed tube. Process until the pastry nearly forms a ball. Remove the dough to a floured surface and form into a disc. Wrap the dough in plastic wrap and refrigerate for one hour.

*I*n the meantime, make the filling. Place all the ingredients for the filling in a small saucepan. Cook, stirring occasionally, over moderate heat until the mixture dries to form a paste. Set aside and allow to cool.

*P*reheat oven to 350 degrees. Line cookie sheets with parchment. Take the chilled pastry and pinch off a piece about the size of a walnut in its shell. On a lightly floured surface, flatten the piece of dough into a small circle. Place a generous teaspoon of filling on top and form the pastry around it shaping it into a nice round ball. Continue with the remaining dough and filling until one or the other is used up, placing the balls on the prepared cookie sheets as they are done. Bake for 25 minutes or until firm. Transfer the balls to cooling racks and allow to cool completely.

*M*elt the chocolate, using a microwave if available. If neccessary, add vegetable oil to the chocolate in droplets to create a good consistency for dipping.

*U*sing two table forks, pick up one of the balls and place it, top side down, in the melted chocolate. Roll it around in the chocolate until the top is completely coated. (Most of the bottom of the balls will get covered also, and that is just fine.) Place the chocolate-dipped balls on a cooling rack. The cooling rack should sit over a plate or wax paper to catch the drips. Allow the cookies to set until the chocolate is firm. They may be refrigerated to speed this process. They will loose their shine, but they still taste great.

Makes approximately (40) 1 1/2 to 2-inch round balls.

K. T.

CINNAMON ICE CREAM

Bring the cream, milk, and syrup to a simmer in a 2-quart saucepan. Place the egg yolks in a medium, heatproof bowl and whisk together briefly. Pour in half the cream mixture very slowly and whisk vigorously to prevent the yolks from curdling! Scrape this mixture back into the pan, and cook over very low heat, stirring constantly, until the custard reaches 165 degrees on an instant read thermometer. Remove from the heat, then stir in the salt. Allow to cool to room temperature. Stir in the cinnamon and chill thoroughly. Freeze in an ice cream maker according to the manufacturer's directions. This is best stored at 0 degrees or below. Place the ice cream in the refrigerator for 15 minutes before serving, as it is really too firm to scoop easily right from the freezer.

Makes about 1 quart.

3 cups heavy cream
1 cup milk
1/2 cup real maple syrup
4 egg yolks
1/2 teaspoon salt
1 1/2 teaspoons ground cinnamon

SOUTH OF THE BORDER SUPPER

"South of the Border, down Mexico way..." are words I remember from a song my father used to sing when I was a young girl. This "South of the Border" menu is presented for celebrating Cinqo de Mayo — the 5th of May — or anytime you feel like some delicious Mexican food — that's quite often if you are anything like us!

Pepper-Jack Cheese Bites
•
Scallop Ceviche
•
Turkey Mole over Rice
•
Pear Crisp

To start the meal, Diane offers Pepper-Jack Cheese Bites. Serve them with a glass of white wine or even a Margarita.

The Scallop Ceviche with its sun-dried tomatoes, and avocado echoes the colors of the Mexican flag.

Dan's Turkey Mole over Rice is a spicy combination of many flavors. The sauce can be prepared ahead of time and the meat added ten minutes before serving. You may want to double the recipe and freeze some for a quick dinner another day.

Our dessert is an interesting variation of a traditional American finale — Pear Crisp. It is served warm with whipped cream or ice cream. This menu is good cause for celebrating anytime of the year!!

Gongia M. Vareldzis

2 eggs
1/2 cup milk
1 cup all-purpose flour
1 cup cracker meal
2 tablespoons baking powder
1 tablespoon dry mustard
1 teaspoon chili powder
1/2 teaspoon coarse salt
1/4 teaspoon freshly ground white pepper
1/2 to 3/4 cup beer
....

Corn oil for deep frying
....

1 pound red pepper jack cheese, cut into 3/4-inch cubes, well chilled

PEPPER-JACK CHEESE BITES

Beat eggs with milk in a medium-sized bowl. In a separate bowl combine the flour, cracker meal, baking powder, mustard, chili powder, salt, and pepper. Stir the dry ingredients into the egg mixture. The mixture will be stiff. Add enough beer to make the batter lumpy and thick. (The batter can be made ahead and refrigerated. Add more beer if the batter becomes too thick.)

Heat the oil to 375 degrees. Dip the cold cheese into the batter, making sure it is coated completely. Deep fry 5 to 6 pieces at a time. When the coating is golden brown on all sides (this only takes about 1 minute*), remove to paper towels and drain well. Serve immediately.

* If the cheese bursts through the coating, you are frying them too long.

Makes about 60 appetizers.

DM

SCALLOP CEVICHE

For this ceviche I have taken my favorite ingredients from a couple of different recipes—scallops and avocados—and added one of my own—sun-dried tomatoes—for this fresh-tasting first course.

Rinse and drain the scallops. Place in a large bowl with the avocado cubes. Add the lime juice and let marinate in the refrigerator for at least two hours. This will "cook" the scallops.

*I*n the meantime, soak the sun-dried tomatoes in hot tap water to cover, for at least 30 minutes. Drain the water. Pat the tomatoes dry with a paper towel and finely julienne.

*J*ust before serving, toss all the other ingredients except the shredded lettuce and the cilantro with the scallops and avocado. Place the shredded lettuce on a large serving platter or on individual first-course plates. Using a slotted spoon place the scallop mixture on top of the lettuce and garnish with the chopped cilantro.

Serves 6.

K. T.

1 pound bay scallops (if using larger scallops, cut in half horizontally)
1 large, ripe avocado, peeled and cut into 1/2-inch cubes
1 cup lime juice, freshly squeezed
1 ounce sun-dried tomatoes, preferably not packed in oil
1 red pepper, seeded and cut into 1/4-inch dice
3 scallions, white part with about 1 inch of green, thinly sliced
2 green Jalapeño chilies, seeded and minced
1 tomato, seeded and diced
3 tablespoons extra virgin olive oil
Coarse salt and freshly ground black pepper, to taste
Shredded lettuce
2 tablespoons cilantro, chopped

1/4 cup olive oil
2 cups diced onion
2 large cloves garlic, minced
· · · · · · · · · · · · · · · · ·
1 tablespoon paprika
1 teaspoon ground pasilla (dark) chili
1/4 teaspoon dried thyme
1/2 teaspoon ground coriander seed
1 teaspoon dried leaf cilantro or 1 tablespoon chopped fresh
1 teaspoon ground cumin
1 1/2 teaspoons ground cinnamon
1/2 teaspoon ground allspice
1 canned chili chipotle, minced (smoked, dried Jalapeño canned in a dark sauce— available in the Mexican foods section in better supermarkets)
1 bay leaf
2 teaspoons coarse salt
2 tablespoons sesame seeds
Few grinds black pepper
1 tablespoon Worcestershire sauce
2 1/4 cups chicken broth
1 15-ounce can white or yellow hominy
1 cup raisins
2 ounces unsweetened chocolate
1 cup coarsely chopped walnuts
· · · · · · · · · · · · · · · · ·
2 pounds turkey breast, cut into 1-inch pieces
1/4 cup diced jicama
Sliced scallion tops for garnish

TURKEY MOLE OVER RICE

In a 4 or 5-quart dutch sauté pan heat the olive oil. Add the onions and garlic and cook over moderate heat, stirring, until the vegetables are soft but not brown.

Stir in the paprika, ground chili, thyme, ground coriander seed, cilantro, cumin, cinnamon, allspice, chili chipotle, bay leaf, salt, sesame seeds, black pepper, Worcestershire, broth, hominy, and raisins. Bring to a simmer and cook slowly, covered, for 15 minutes. Stir in the chocolate and walnuts and adjust the salt if necessary.

Ten minutes before serving, stir in the turkey and cook, covered, just until the meat is cooked. Do not overcook or the meat will become dry! Stir in the jicama.

Serve over rice, garnished with the sliced scallions.

Serves 8 to 10.

PEAR CRISP

Fruit crisp, especially apple and pear, has always been one of my children's favorite desserts. We love it served very warm with ice cream. You can also use sweetened whipped cream or frozen yogurt. I've adapted the recipe for "adults" here by adding pear brandy and nuts, but I think it still appeals to the child in us all! I use firm, ripe pears such as Anjou or Bosc. You can also use Comice, but Bartletts are too soft to hold their shape well.

Combine the flour, rolled oats, and brown sugar together with the spices in a bowl. Cut in the 6 tablespoons of butter as you would for a pie crust until the mixture is crumbly. Fold in the nuts and set aside.

Peel the pears and cut into slices about 1/4-inch thick. Layer in a single layer in a 12x7 inch baking dish (preferably glass). Sprinkle with lemon juice, then brandy. Dot with the 2 tablespoons of butter.

Distribute the crumb mixture evenly over top of the fruit. Bake at 350 degrees until nicely browned on top and the fruit feels soft when pierced with a fork, about 30 to 40 minutes. Serve warm.

Serves 8.

*A wonderful Pear William brandy is made by Clear Creek Distillery in Portland, Oregon.

1 cup all-purpose flour
1/2 cup rolled oats (quick-cooking)
1/2 cup brown sugar
1 teaspoon ground nutmeg
1/2 teaspoon ground cinnamon
1/2 teaspoon ground cardamom
6 tablespoons unsalted butter
1/2 cup chopped pecans
. . . .
6-8 firm, ripe Anjou or Bosc pears
. . . .
1 tablespoon lemon juice
2 tablespoons Pear William* brandy, or any white, clear liqueur such as Cointreau, Triple Sec, or Curaçao
2 tablespoons unsalted butter

DAD'S DAY BOURBON BREAKFAST

Bourbon for breakfast? What is this world—and perhaps more to the point, this cookbook—coming to? So let's get this straight: this book is about flavors—good ones. One of the "good ones" is a unique American whiskey: bourbon.

If the idea of using a distilled spirit for flavor in cooking bothers you, it might interest you to know that the little bottles of "flavor" and "extract" sitting on your pantry shelves are frequently about 35 percent alcohol! The fact is that alcohol is a solvent—that is, it leaches flavor out of food. In cooking, the alcohol evaporates leaving behind a flavor residue. Cognac, an altogether special French brandy, has been used by some very savvy French chefs for generations. An interesting footnote to this discussion is that a very fine French cook and author of our acquaintance, Madeleine Kamman, specifies a famous Tennessee whiskey in a number of her recipes! Bourbon and nearly identical whiskies from Tennessee and elsewhere pack quite a flavor punch.

So never mind handing Dad two or three fingers of his favorite over ice! What we have here is a menu with a number of recipes that use bourbon as a flavor enhancer. For the best, most undiluted flavor we suggest "straight" rather than blended. Kathleen's Creamy Bourbon Orangeade won't knock your guests out, it will just make them smile and lick their lips. My Bourbon Sticky Buns use the whiskey for its inherent round, slightly sweet flavor which mingles oh so well with butter, pecans, brown sugar, and good chocolate!

So tell Dad that a couple of hundred years of lively distilling history (what with tax rebellions, revenuers, and all) is all wrapped up in a neat little package called Dad's Bourbon Breakfast!

Dan Taggart

3 cups fresh-squeezed orange juice

1 1/2 cups half and half

1/2 teaspoon ground fresh nutmeg

1 tablespoon finely chopped, grated orange peel

1 tablespoon sugar

3/4 cup bourbon whiskey

CREAMY BOURBON ORANGEADE

Blend all ingredients in a covered jar. Shake well to blend. Chill for at least 2 hours or overnight. Serve over ice. Garnish with grated nutmeg if desired.

Serves 6 to 8.

K. T.

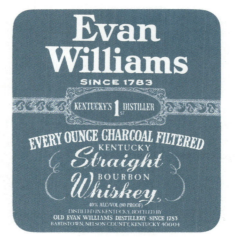

SAVORY FRITTATA

Beat the eggs well with an electric beater, blending in the cream. Stir in the turkey, Gorgonzola, tomatoes, and freshly ground pepper, to taste. Snip the basil leaves into small pieces and add to the egg mixture. Add the green onions and parmesan.

Set the oven rack about 6-inches beneath the broiler. Preheat the broiler.

On top of the stove, melt the butter in a heavy, 9 to 10-inch cast-iron skillet. When the butter has melted and starts to sizzle, add the egg mixture. Cook over medium heat without stirring until the bottom and sides are set and the bottom begins to brown. Remove from the stove and immediately place under the broiler. Cook until the frittata puffs and begins to brown on top. The center will still be soft. If you like your eggs more set than that, leave it under the broiler a little longer, but be careful it doesn't dry out and get tough.

Cut into wedge-shaped pieces and serve immediately.

Serves 6 to 8.

10 eggs
1/4 cup cream
4 ounces smoked turkey, diced
4 ounces Gorgonzola cheese, crumbled
2 ounces sun-dried tomatoes, minced
Freshly ground black pepper, to taste
6 large fresh basil leaves
3 green onions, thinly sliced
1 tablespoon Parmesan cheese, grated
3 tablespoons butter

4 large russet potatoes, peeled
1 medium onion, peeled
Coarse salt, to taste
Freshly ground black pepper, to taste
1/4 cup freshly minced parsley*
. . . .
3 tablespoons bacon fat, additional, if needed

DOUG MORGAN'S FAVORITE HASH BROWNS

During our last visit to San Francisco, I consulted with my brother-in-law about hash browns. Doug is a self-proclaimed hash brown expert. It is his mission to taste all made. I was told that hash browns must have some onion and must be cooked in bacon fat...“But what about cholesterol and healthy eating?” I exclaimed. Doug's retort was, “Not when it comes to hash browns.” So, for Father's Day, which Doug is now entitled to celebrate, I give you Doug's version of hash browns. (I have taken the liberty of adding a bit of minced parsley for interest.)

Grate the potatoes, place in a colander, and rinse well with cold water. Squeeze them gently, then pat dry with paper towels. Grate the onion and mix with the potatoes in a medium-sized bowl. Season with salt** and pepper and blend in the minced parsley. If you are not planning to fry the hash browns right away, then cover the potato mixture by placing plastic wrap directly on top of the potatoes to prevent them from browning.

*H*eat a large cast-iron or other heavy-bottomed skillet on medium-high heat for several minutes. Add the bacon fat. Form the hash browns into either 3-inch pancakes or rectangles and fry until crisp and golden brown. Turn the pancakes and fry on the other side. Drain and serve hot. Keep warm in a 275 degree oven while frying additional batches.

Serves 6.

* I like to use flat leaf Italian parsley if available. The flavor is much more pronounced than the more standard curly leaf parsley.

** If you are mixing the hash browns in advance then wait and add the salt just before frying. The salt will leech water from the potatoes while it sits.

DM

DAN'S BOURBON STICKY BUNS

I find most sticky buns (or cinnamon rolls or whatever you are inclined to call them) not worth eating. They are often gigantic dough balls made with too much sugar and "butter-flavored" margarine and too few nuts. Having now set myself up to be smartly knocked down, I nonetheless offer up these rolls. They are aromatic with orange zest; rich with butter, pecans, and chocolate; and I hope not too sweet. I have designed this recipe to make six good-sized buns. They just so happen to fit perfectly in the Texas-sized muffin pans so popular of late. If you don't have a muffin pan put three rolls in each of two medium bread pans.

Mix the warm milk and brown sugar together and stir in the yeast. Allow to rest until foamy, about 5 minutes. Stir in the salt. In the workbowl of a food processor fitted with the metal blade, place the flour, butter (cut into tablespoon-sized bits), and orange zest (the colored part of the rind.) Run the machine until these ingredients are well blended.

With the machine running, slowly pour in the milk mixture until a dough ball forms. If the dough sticks to the side of the workbowl, add more flour by the tablespoonful. Allow the dough to revolve (knead) in the machine for 45 seconds. Remove the dough to a gallon-sized plastic bag, squeeze out all the air, and place a wire twist at the *top* of the bag so that the dough has room to expand. Allow the dough to rise until nearly doubled in size.

In a bowl, place the melted butter, brown sugar, chopped pecans, and cinnamon. Stir together. Remove the dough from the bag. On a lightly floured countertop, roll it out into an 8x9-inch rectangle. Spread the butter/nut mixture over all but a 1-inch strip of the dough. Sprinkle on the chocolate chips. Moisten the plain edge of the dough with water and roll the dough up toward that plain edge to create a cylinder. Pinch the seam tightly and use your hands to create a uniformly-shaped log, about 9 inches long.

Grease the muffin pan. In the bottom of the muffin cups place the remaining chopped nuts and brown sugar. Measure in the bourbon. Pour on the butter. Cut the dough into six pieces with a serrated knife. Press each piece out to fit the muffin tin and place the circles of dough in the pan. Cover with plastic wrap and allow to rise until just a little below the top of the pan. Preheat the oven to 375 degrees.

Place the muffin tin on a baking sheet with sides, in case of overflowing butter/bourbon mixture. Bake about 30 minutes or until an instant read thermometer registers at least 180 degrees. Allow to cool 5 minutes, then invert the rolls onto a serving plate.

Makes 6.

2/3 cup milk, 105 to 115 degrees
1/3 cup brown sugar
1 tablespoon yeast
1/2 teaspoon salt
2 1/4 cups all-purpose unbleached flour, approximately
2 ounces (1/2 stick) unsalted butter
Grated zest of 1 orange
....

4 tablespoons unsalted butter, melted
2 tablespoons brown sugar
3/4 cup medium chopped pecans
1 teaspoon ground cinnamon
1/3 cup semisweet chocolate chips (such as Guittard)
....

6 tablespoons medium chopped pecans
6 tablespoons brown sugar
6 tablespoons bourbon whiskey
2 tablespoons melted butter

SUMMER ELEGANCE

I don't always have the urge to cook a lovely, multicourse dinner in the summer, when the thought of sunning by the pool or working in the garden has more appeal. But sometimes, if friends I haven't seen for awhile are arriving from out-of-town, then, sure enough, I find myself planning a dinner party.

Poppy Seed Pasta with
Toasted Walnut Butter
•
Sautéed Chicken with a
Shiitake Mushroom
Beurre Blanc
•
Two-Color Squash
Sauté
•
Mixed Green Salad
Vinaigrette
•
Berry Filo Napoleon

Because my friends know that I'm a cook, they expect me to produce an elaborate menu. That doesn't mean I will slave in the kitchen for days, but I am likely to serve a menu that has several new and different combinations.

For example, the menu we present here has all the trappings of a perfect dinner party. The Poppy Seed Pasta with Toasted Walnut Butter is wonderful. The first time it was presented to the "cookbook group," it was a keeper. In fact, we didn't have one criticism. The pasta is unusual and the sauce complements it beautifully.

The Sautéed Chicken with a Shiitake Mushroom Beurre Blanc was a dish I created for my husband and myself when I happened to have some boneless chicken breasts left over. I refined the sauce and rewrote the recipe to serve 8. This is elegant food with rich and heady tastes. Dan's Two-Color Squash Sauté is a simple accompaniment with crisp-fried onions as the topping.

I always want a salad after the entrée – it gives me just the right break so that dessert seems all the more appealing! For this salad I suggest using red leaf lettuce, arugula, and large mushrooms. Buy what looks the best, but try to have at least one of the greens a bit spicy and sharp. The enoki mushrooms are a fun garnish if available.

Georgia, who adores working with filo dough, has created a luscious Napoleon using filo instead of puff pastry. This dessert has several components which make it look complicated, but, because everything can be done ahead, the final assembly is really quite simple. Your guests will be won over.

When planning a dinner party, I try to look for recipes that I can do, at least in part, in advance. With this menu, I would make the pasta, wash the lettuces, clean and prepare some of the vegetables, and make the custard the day before. On the morning of the party I would finish getting ingredients together for the sauces, and make the filo layers for the dessert. Then, with that much done ahead, I am able to cook and enjoy the party as well.

Now, about the wine. A spicy California Gewürztraminer or a Riesling would be great with the pasta. Then I suggest an oaky Chardonnay or a Beaujolais with the entrée. The earthiness of the mushrooms makes these wines very appealing to me.

Serve dessert on the patio, enjoy the cool summer evening breezes and good conversation with friends.

Diane f Morgan

POPPY SEED PASTA WITH TOASTED WALNUT BUTTER

Place all ingredients in the workbowl of a food processor fitted with the metal blade. Blend until the pasta dough holds together. Roll out with a hand crank or electric pasta machine. Cut into fettucine shape. Set aside. Bring six to seven quarts of salted water to a boil. Meanwhile, prepare the following sauce.

Melt the butter in a small saucepan. Add the lemon juice. In another small, heavy-gauge skillet place the crushed cumin seeds over medium heat. Stir and shake until they just begin to brown. Add the walnuts and continue stirring and shaking until walnuts are lightly toasted.

When the pasta water has come to a boil, cook the pasta very briefly until al dente. (It should take one to two minutes at most.) Drain the pasta well in a colander. Toss immediately with the hot lemon butter and then the toasted walnut mixture. Divide the pasta among eight salad-size plates. Give each portion a generous grinding of fresh pepper and garnish with cherry tomatoes or yellow tomatoes and parsley.

Makes 8 first-course servings.

K. T.

1 cup semolina flour
1 cup all-purpose flour
1/3 cup (2 ounces) poppy seeds
2 teaspoons salt
2 large eggs
1/4 cup, or more, water
. . . .
SAUCE
6 ounces (1 1/2 sticks) unsalted butter
2 tablespoons fresh lemon juice
1 teaspoon crushed cumin seeds
1/2 cup chopped walnuts
. . . .
Freshly ground black pepper
Cherry tomatoes or yellow tomatoes, for garnish
Parsley, for garnish

7 skinless, boneless chicken breasts,
tenderloin removed
4 tablespoons clarified butter
Salt, to taste
Freshly ground white pepper, to taste

. . . .

1/2 pound Shiitake mushrooms
2 tablespoons unsalted butter

. . . .

1/3 cup sherry wine vinegar
1/3 cup dry white wine
1/3 cup chicken stock
2 shallots, finely minced
2 sticks unsalted butter, room temperature
Coarse salt, freshly ground white pepper and
sugar, to taste
2 tablespoons finely minced fresh parsley

. . . .

Fresh watercress for garnish

SAUTÉED CHICKEN WITH A SHIITAKE MUSHROOM BEURRE BLANC

Using a very sharp paring knife remove the tendon from each of the tenderloins. Cut each of the chicken breasts into four pieces, resembling the shape of the tenderloins. Refrigerate covered until ready to sauté.

Remove the stems from the mushrooms and discard. With a slightly moistened paper towel wipe the mushrooms clean. Slice thinly and reserve covered.

Up to one hour prior to serving the entrée you can sauté the mushrooms over high heat in 2 tablespoons of butter. Sauté just until the mushrooms give up their liquid and begin to brown. Remove from the heat and reserve. (I sauté the mushrooms in the same pan used for sautéing the chicken).

In a medium-sized sauté pan, combine the sherry wine vinegar, white wine, chicken stock, and shallots. Bring to a boil and reduce to 1/4 cup. Off the heat whisk in the butter, 2 tablespoons at a time, blending well after each addition. Adjust to taste with salt, a little sugar, and freshly ground white pepper. Stir in the minced parsley and keep warm while sautéing the chicken, but do not let the sauce boil.

Have the entrée plates warm but not hot. (If the plates are hot the sauce is likely to separate.)

Heat a large sauté pan oven medium high-heat. Add 3 tablespoons of the clarified butter. When hot, add the chicken pieces to the pan and sauté in batches, keeping the pieces separated. Allow 1-2 minutes per side, but do not overcook. Keep the cooked chicken pieces warm while you are sautéing the remaining batches.

To serve, place four chicken pieces in a petal arrangement on the plate. Spoon some of the sauce over the chicken and scatter some of the mushrooms over the top. Garnish with fresh watercress and serve immediately.

Serves 8.

DM

TWO-COLOR SQUASH SAUTÉ

This is a sauté of both green and yellow zucchini, using some of the colorful peel as garnish. It is topped with crisp-fried onions of the sort common to Indian cuisine.

In a large, heavy sauté pan heat the oil over medium to medium-high heat. Add the sliced onion and cook, stirring frequently. Continue cooking the onion until it turns nearly black but does not actually burn. Just when you think the onion is about to be cremated, lift it out with a slotted spoon and drain on two layers of paper towels. Remove the pan from the heat while you prepare the zucchini.

Use a vegetable peeler to remove the skin of one of each color squash in long strips. Set those aside. Cut the peeled and unpeeled squashes in coin shapes about 1/4-inch thick.

Add oil to the pan, if necessary, to equal about 2 to 3 tablespoons. Heat the pan until the oil nearly smokes and toss in the squash coins and basil. Cook, tossing or stirring, until the squash is just crisp-tender. Season with salt and pepper and toss again. Remove the squash to a serving plate. Toss the skin strips into the hot pan and quickly stir-fry them until their color brightens and they soften just slightly. Remove the pan from the heat and spread the strips over the sautéed coins. Top with the crisp-fried onions and serve.

Serves 8.

1/4 cup vegetable oil
1 large, sweet onion, peeled and thinly sliced
2 small to medium green zucchini
2 small to medium yellow zucchini
1 tablespoon dried basil
Salt and freshly ground black pepper, to taste

2 tablespoons balsamic vinegar
6 tablespoons extra virgin olive oil
1/4 teaspoon sugar
1/2 teaspoon coarse salt
Freshly ground black pepper, to taste
1 1/2 tablespoons freshly minced parsley
. . . .
9 large mushrooms, wiped clean, then thinly sliced
1 large head red leaf lettuce, cleaned and dried
1/2 bunch arugula, cleaned (leaving about 2-inches of stem intake) and dried
1 package enoki mushrooms, stems cut 1/2-inch from the bottom

MIXED GREEN SALAD VINAIGRETTE

In a large salad bowl mix the vinegar, olive oil, sugar, salt, and pepper. Stir well to combine. Add the freshly minced parsley. Mix well and taste. Adjust the seasonings if needed.

About 20 minutes before serving add the sliced mushrooms to the dressing. Toss well and let marinate.

When ready to serve the salad, tear the lettuce into bite-size pieces and add to the salad bowl along with the arugula which should be left whole. Toss to combine. Divide among the salad plates and garnish each plate with the enoki mushrooms.

Serves 6 .

DM

BERRY FILO NAPOLEON

Make the custard first and refrigerate. Heat milk to scald (until a skin forms and it begins to boil over). Mix cornstarch and sugar in a medium-sized sauce pan. Mix egg yolks with a fork to even out. When milk is ready, pour half over the cornstarch mixture and whisk until smooth. Add yolks and whisk a few times. Add the remaining milk and whisk to combine. Heat, whisking constantly, until it thickens—about a minute. Remove from the heat and whisk in butter. Allow to cool about 2-3 minutes and add the Grand Marnier. In order to keep a "skin" from forming on top, press plastic wrap directly on top of the custard when covering, rather than on top of the pan.

*L*ayer the sheets of filo one directly on top of the other, buttering between each layer. Cut into four even strips about 4-inches wide. Use two buttered or non-stick cookie sheets and place two strips on each pan. Bake at 350 degrees until golden brown, about 12-15 minutes. Remove to a cooling rack and cool completely.

When ready to assemble, whip the cream with the powdered sugar until stiff. Mix half the whipped cream into the custard, using a whisk to make sure it is smooth. Place a strip of filo on a serving plate and spread with 1/3 of the custard. Add another strip and repeat. Do the same with the third strip. Place the fourth strip on the top and brush with the melted jelly (this is the "glue" that holds the fruit in place). Pipe the remaining cream on the top for decoration, forming squares or triangles and fill in with the fruit. Refrigerate until ready to serve and the dessert is set. Using a sharp serrated knife, cut into slices and serve.

Serves 6 to 8, depending on how thick you cut the slices.

Note: The custard can be prepared one day in advance and kept refrigerated. The pastry can be baked earlier the same day and set aside. Assemble up to two hours before serving and refrigerate. It does not keep well if you refrigerate it overnight, as the pastry becomes soggy.

CUSTARD
1 cup whole milk
2 tablespoons cornstarch
1/4 cup superfine sugar
2 egg yolks
1 tablespoons unsalted butter, room temperature
1 tablespoon Grand Marnier, or other flavoring

· · · · · · · · · · · · · · · · ·

9 sheets filo dough
6 tablespoons unsalted butter, melted

· · · · · · · · · · · · · · · · ·

1 cup whipping cream
1/4 cup powdered sugar
1/4 cup strawberry, apricot, or currant jelly, melted

· · · · · · · · · · · · · · · · ·

FRUIT FOR DECORATING THE TOP: raspberries, blueberries, strawberries, or any seasonal fruit.

A BRIDAL LUNCHEON

**Marinated Melon
with Prosciutto
"Streamers"**

•

Caesar Salad

•

Herbed Brioche

•

**Frozen Strawberry
Souffle**

•

Sand Tart Hearts

*L*et's see, it was 11 years ago this spring that a multitude of bridal luncheons were given in my honor. Several were catered, one was in a friend's home, and though all were lovely, the food served at them was less than memorable. Now I'm not being an ingrate, it's just that good food can enhance a celebration immeasurably, and to pass up a golden opportunity, such as a bridal luncheon, is clearly a mistake. So, this group of cooks put on their best thinking caps to arrange a glorious, never-to-be-forgotten luncheon for the bride-to-be.

This food has character, quality, and an artful presentation. We begin by marrying the classic combination of melon and prosciutto in a new way. The melon is marinated in a white wine mixture and garnished with chopped pistachios. This makes a splendid appetizer.

For the entrée, we offer a Caesar Salad "dressed" to perfection. To accompany the salad, Dan, using his bread-making skills, has made an Herbed Brioche. It contains lots of butter, eggs, and basil and makes a tasty replacement for dinner rolls or french bread.

My Frozen Strawberry Souffle is pretty in pink and long in berry flavor. Adding some Grand Marnier enhances the flavor further. Serve the souffle in individual ramekins for a lovely presentation. To accompany the frozen souffle, Georgia offers a recipe for Sand Tart Hearts. These crisp, thin cookies are cut into heart shapes and sprinkled with fine, red sugar crystals.

A toast to the upcoming celebration, with a marriage of flavors as delicate as the bride and as hearty as the groom!!!

Diane F. Morgan

2 large, ripe melons

2 cups slightly sweet white wine

······················

12 very thin slices of prosciutto

1/2 cup pistachio nuts, toasted and chopped

MARINATED MELON WITH PROSCIUTTO

You can use any melons you like in this first course, but it is more attractive if you use two with different colors, such as cantaloupe and honeydew. Have the prosciutto sliced very thin. I like to use a slightly sweet wine for the marinade, such as a German Spatlese, but you can use a drier wine if that suits your taste.

Peel the melons and cut in half lengthwise. Slice into 1/4-inch slices and place in a single layer in two large, glass baking dishes. Pour the wine over the melon and marinate in the refrigerator overnight.

*T*he next day, remove the slices from the marinade, reserving the wine. Arrange four slices of the melon in alternating colors on a plate. (A glass salad plate is perfect.)

Slice the prosciutto lengthwise into long strips about 1/8-inch wide. Lay the strips of prosciutto over the melon in a decorative pattern. Sprinkle with a teaspoon of the chopped pistachio nuts.

Serves 12.

2 large garlic cloves

4 tablespoons freshly-squeezed lemon juice

2 large eggs

2 tablespoons anchovy paste

1/2 teaspoon freshly ground black pepper

1 cup extra virgin olive oil

2 large heads romaine lettuce

4 ounces Parmigiano-Reggiano or other fine-quality, dry grating cheese

8 ounces homemade croutons (see introduction)

CAESAR SALAD

There is no question that this is one of my favorite salads and, it seems, almost everyone else's as well. Part of why it is wonderful is its simplicity! But like many simple creations, its success depends on the quality of the ingredients used. For instance, I feel homemade croutons are a must. I don't mean that you need to use homemade bread (although it is nice). A good-quality storebought loaf will do. Cut the bread into 1/2-inch cubes and dry them in a 250 degree oven for 30 to 40 minutes. It is always wise to test the croutons after about 30 minutes in the oven to make sure they are not becoming rock hard. After the croutons have been dried and cooled, they can be placed in an airtight bag and stored for days before making the salad. The recipe below makes a large quantity of the salad, but it can easily be halved for smaller groups or for just yourself and your sweetie.

To make the dressing, peel the garlic cloves and place them in the workbowl of a food processor fitted with a metal blade. Process until the garlic is well chopped. Add the lemon juice, eggs, anchovy paste, and black pepper. Process again briefly to blend the ingredients. With the machine running pour the olive oil through the feed tube in a steady stream. Dressing may be prepared a few days in advance.

When ready to serve the salad, tear the romaine into bite-sized pieces. Wash and spin in a salad spinner and place in a very large bowl. Grate the cheese, and add it along with the croutons to the bowl. Dizzle about 3/4 of the dressing over the greens. Add more, if neccessary. The greens should be coated but not soggy. The rest of the dressing will keep well for another week. Serve on individual plates.

Makes 12 servings.

K. T.

HERBED BRIOCHE

Ah, brioche! An ethereal combination of flour, butter, and eggs, brioche is to white bread what Baccarat crystal is to everyday glassware. It is rich and light, all at the same time! In this version I've added basil since it goes so well with this menu.

I like to bake this as one large, round loaf. I use a 3 1/2-quart or larger saucepan with an oven proof handle as my baking pan. This produces a cylindrical loaf with a rounded top. But you can make this in any shape you like, using regular loaf pans or little brioche molds. The instructions are for a food processor of 8-cup capacity or greater. If you use a stand mixer, allow the dough to go through its first rise without the addition of the butter, then drizzle in the warm (not hot) melted butter while running the machine on low speed. Then proceed as written.

Mix together the yeast, sugar, and water. Allow this mixture to stand until foamy, about 5 minutes. Meanwhile, crack 5 large eggs (room temperature) into a 2-cup liquid measure. If the volume is less than 1 1/4 cups, add milk to make up the difference. Beat the eggs, milk, and yeast mixture together in the measure. Stir in the salt.

In the workbowl of a food processor fitted with the *metal* blade place, the flour and *cold* butter which has been cut in tablespoon-size pieces. Run the machine until the butter has been incorporated into the flour. Remove the metal blade and insert the dough blade.

Stir the sugar and basil into the yeast/egg mixture. Have extra flour on the counter ready to add to the machine if the dough is too sticky to revolve inside the workbowl. With the machine running slowly, pour the liquids into the flour mixture. When a ball of dough forms and begins to rotate inside the machine, allow this "kneading" to continue for about 45 seconds, adding flour as necessary to control stickiness. Remove the dough from the machine, and place it in a gallon-size plastic bag with all the air squeezed out and a wire twist placed at the *top* of the bag so the dough has room to expand. Place the dough in a warm place to rise until doubled. This may take from one to several hours depending on temperature.

When the dough has doubled in size, remove it from the bag, shape it into a large ball, and place it in a greased, straight-sided saucepan of 3 1/2-quart or more capacity. Cover with a towel or oiled plastic wrap and allow to rise until nearly triple its original size. Preheat the oven to 425 degrees.

Carefully brush the top of the loaf with the beaten egg. Bake for 10 minutes, reduce the heat to 350 degrees, and bake until an instant read thermometer registers at least 180 degrees, approximately 35 to 45 more minutes. Cover the top with foil if it begins to brown too much during baking.

Allow the bread to cool in the pan for 5 to 10 minutes. Then run an icing spatula or other straight-bladed tool around the loaf to loosen it, and invert the pan to knock out the brioche. Cool on a rack.

Serves 10 to 12.

1 tablespoon, or 1 package active dry yeast
1/2 teaspoon sugar
1/4 cup warm water, about 105 degrees
5 large eggs plus enough milk, if necessary, to equal 1 1/4 cups liquid
2 teaspoons coarse salt
4 cups all-purpose unbleached flour, approximately
6 ounces (1 1/2 sticks) unsalted butter, cold
3 tablespoons sugar
2 tablespoons dried basil, or 1/3 cup chopped fresh

. . . .

GLAZE
1 egg, beaten

FROZEN STRAWBERRY SOUFFLE

1 1/2 pints strawberries, cleaned and stems removed
4 tablespoons Grand Marnier
....

1 1/2 cups sugar
1 cup water
....

4 egg whites, room temperature
1/2 teaspoon coarse salt
....

3 cups whipping cream, well chilled
2 teaspoons vanilla

This dessert is light, creamy, and rich with the flavors of strawberry and Grand Marnier. I think it is the perfect finish to a Bridal Luncheon.

Cut the strawberries into quarters, then purée using a food processor. Combine the strawberry purée with the Grand Marnier in a small mixing bowl and reserve at room temperature.

Combine the sugar and water in a medium-sized saucepan and bring to a boil over medium-high heat. Boil until the sugar syrup reaches 235 degrees on a candy thermometer. Remove from the heat.

Place the egg whites and salt in a mixer bowl and beat on high speed until the egg whites form soft peaks. With the mixer running, pour the sugar syrup in a slow steady stream into the beaten egg whites. Stop the mixer and reserve this Italian meringue.

Using another mixer bowl, beat the whipping cream and vanilla on high speed until soft peaks form. If you only have one large bowl to your mixer then gently place the Italian meringue in a large mixing bowl.

Gently fold the strawberry mixture into the Italian meringue. Now fold in the whipped cream. When all has been well blended, use a large spoon to fill individual souffle dishes. Mound the mixture at the top, as if it were a finished baked souffle. Place the dishes on a tray and freeze for at least 4 hours before serving. These may be made several days ahead.

Let stand at room temperature about ten minutes before serving.

Makes 10 to 12 individual souffles, using 3 1/4-inch ramekins.

DM

SAND TART HEARTS

These cookies are an old family favorite. The dough must be frozen overnight and it is delicate to work with. You must flour the surface well when you roll them out. They can be rerolled once or twice, but after that the dough becomes difficult and breaks apart.

1/2 pound unsalted butter, room temperature
1 cup sugar
2 eggs
1/4 teaspoon ground mace
4 cups all-purpose flour

Save most of the white of one egg to brush on the tops before baking. In an electric mixer, beat the butter until it turns white and is very soft and fluffy. Add the sugar gradually, beating continuously. Add the egg and yolk of the second one, beating well. Mix the mace with the flour and add gradually on low speed until incorporated into the dough.

Knead the dough slightly with your hands to form a smooth lump of dough. Wrap in plastic wrap and then foil and freeze overnight.

Remove from the freezer when ready to bake and allow to stand for a short time. Taking one small portion at a time, roll out very thin. (I make them about 1/16 to 1/8-inch thick). Cut into heart shapes with a fluted cutter and place on an ungreased nonstick cookie sheet. Beat the egg white slightly with a fork or whisk, and brush on the tops of the cookies with a narrow pastry brush. Sprinkle the top with a little sugar. Bake at 375 degrees for about 10 to 12 minutes until the cookies are golden but not too brown.

As an option, you can place half a pecan or half a blanched almond in the center of the cookies.

This recipe makes approximately 120 cookies. It can be doubled quite easily by using three eggs instead of two.

FOURTH OF JULY BARBECUE

"As American as barbecued ribs" –

We can add this adage to the Mom and apple pie combo. Certainly on the Fourth of July few things are as American as a big slab of ribs. The ribs Dan has devised for this celebration menu are Smoked Country Ribs. They are thick, succulent, and permeated with the flavor of mesquite or maple smoke. In another fine salute to summer's food glories, Diane has created a Cajun Corn Salad to heap next to those ribs. We're talking color here – bright yellow corn and zesty green and red peppers. She offers another salad accompaniment for the meal with a crispy Apple Cabbage Slaw.

Smoked Country Ribs
•
Down-Home Baked Beans
•
Apple Cabbage Slaw
•
Cajun Corn Salad
•

But we're not done yet. Dan has developed his favorite version of savory baked beans – slow cooked and aromatic. Now we've got to finish a menu like this with a homey, comforting dessert. I've tried my "darndest" to do this by recreating another recipe from my childhood, Raisin Bread Pudding.

Drinks for this firecracker of a meal might include ice cold beer. But for the few, like myself, who have never acquired a taste for the brew, a good jug red or white wine, or homemade lemonade are the order of the day.

Kathleen Taggart

SMOKED COUNTRY RIBS

When the word "barbecue" is mentioned, many of us imagine streams of hickory, mesquite, or maple smoke sneaking out from under the lid of a backyard grill. Real smoke adds a terrific flavor to lots of foods, as the burgeoning popularity of computer-controlled supermarket smokerooms testifies! Fortunately we backyard "smokers" don't need computers—just some hardwood chips; a charcoal, gas, or electric grill with a cover; and an hour or two.

The tricks are few: soak the wood chips for at least 30 minutes before using so that they smoke before they burn up; arrange a way to catch drippings so that no flare-ups occur; and regulate the heat so that the food cooks slowly enough for the smoke to do its job! Most foods can be smoked in two hours or less. I own a Ducane gas grill with a separate rotisserie burner at the rear. By placing a pan of water under the turning food, I can prevent flare-ups. You can accomplish the same thing with kettle-style grills by placing a pan of water under the food to be cooked, usually below the top grate. Simply bank the charcoal around the pan. Before placing food on the grill, add a small handful of wood chips to the fire. When using a gas grill, put the *soaked* chips in a small, disposable aluminum pan and place it directly on the "lava" rocks. Whichever type of grill you use, close the top of the grill to trap as much smoke as possible! Using medium to low heat, cook the food about as long as it would take to bake in a low oven. Use a thermometer if you're not sure. Add more soaked wood chips once or twice more during the cooking process.

*T*he soy sauce adds saltiness and enhances color. Use it if you like, brushing a little over all surfaces of the ribs. Smoke the ribs until they are cooked but not dried out, approximately 1 1/2 hours over low to medium heat. Serve hot or at room temperature. The leftovers—if any!—can be used in any recipe calling for smoked meat.

DOWN-HOME BAKED BEANS

Bean cookery is usually fairly simple. After an overnight soak (or a 1-hour "hot" soak in a covered pot after an initial boil), small white beans take about an hour to cook in a covered pot and a little less than 30 minutes in a pressure cooker. These baked beans call for nothing extraordinary and will leave you licking your lips! They bake slowly in the oven, leaving you time to do other fun things.

Rinse the beans in a colander under cold running water, discarding any stones or foreign material. Bring the beans to a boil in a large saucepan, turn off the heat, and allow the beans to sit in the hot water for one hour, covered. You can use a pressure cooker instead, cooking the beans for 5 minutes after reaching maximum pressure. Pour off the liquid from this "precooking."

Place the soaked or precooked beans in a large, heavy saucepan of at least 3 1/2-quart capacity. Add one of the onions, quartered, the bay leaf, and enough water to cover by an inch or more. Bring the beans to a boil, reduce to a simmer, and cook until tender but not mushy, about 1 hour. Drain and reserve the cooking liquid.

Mix 2 1/4 cups of the bean liquid with the salt, molasses, brown sugar, mustard, catsup, worcestershire, and pepper.

In a large bowl, gently mix the beans with the flavored liquid and bacon pieces. Cut the remaining onion in half, stick each half with a whole clove, and place the onion halves in the bottom of a baking dish or bean pot of at least 2-quart capacity. Cover with the beans. Add a little more liquid if the beans seem dry. Bake in a 275 degree oven for 5 to 8 hours. Add more bean liquid or water during the baking if the beans become too dry on top.

Serves 8 to 10.

1 pound dry white beans such as navy or great northern
2 medium onions
1 bay leaf
1 teaspoon coarse salt
1/4 cup dark molasses
1/4 cup dark brown sugar
1 1/2 tablespoons Dijon-style mustard
1/4 cup tomato catsup
2 teaspoon worcestershire sauce
6 grinds black pepper or to taste
4 slices bacon, cut in 1-inch pieces
2 whole cloves

1/2 small (1 1/2-pound) head red cabbage

1/2 small (1 1/2-pound) head white cabbage

3 Granny Smith apples, peeled, cored, and julienned

....

Finely grated peel from 1 lemon

1/2 cup (about 2 lemons) freshly squeezed lemon juice

1 cup olive oil

1 teaspoon coarse salt

1 tablespoon sugar

Freshly ground black pepper, to taste

3 tablespoons freshly minced mint

APPLE CABBAGE SLAW

Unlike many cabbage salads that age gracefully, this slaw is really at its best when it is served about one hour after mixing. That isn't to say that all preparation has to be last minute; in fact, the cabbage and apple can be cut earlier in the day and the dressing can be made separately. An hour before serving, combine it all. This salad is refreshing and a perfect complement to the smoked pork.

Cut the core from each of the cabbage halves. Reserve the other halves for later use. With the flat side of the cabbage on a cutting board, slice the cabbage into long thin strips. In a large mixing bowl, toss the two cabbages together. Toss the julienned apple with about 1 tablespoon of the lemon juice, then add to the cabbage. Toss all together, cover, and refrigerate until one hour before serving.

*I*n a jar with a tight-fitting lid, combine the grated lemon peel, lemon juice, olive oil, seasonings, and mint. Stir well to combine. Taste and adjust the flavors. Refrigerate until about 2 hours before serving. Bring to room temperature before tossing with the cabbage.

When ready to toss the slaw, combine the cabbage-apple mixture with the dressing. Taste and adjust flavors once again and reserve until ready to serve.

Serves 8.

DM

1 pound frozen whole kernel corn

1/2 large green pepper, diced

1/2 large sweet red pepper, diced

1/2 small onion, diced

1/2 cup Cajun Mayonnaise, see page 160

1/4 cup sour cream

1 teaspoon sugar

1 teaspoon coarse salt

1 tablespoon minced fresh tarragon

CAJUN CORN SALAD

Use the recipe for Cajun Mayonnaise that accompanies the Shrimp Poached in Beer. This corn salad has some of the basic ingredients of a midwestern corn relish, but I have replaced the typical sweet and sour flavors with Cajun seasonings and fresh tarragon. Double the recipe if you wish and make it for a crowd. The flavors are at their best about two hours after combining, but the salad will keep for a couple of days.

Blanch the corn for 1 minute in a large pot of unsalted boiling water. Drain in a colander and rinse immediately under cold water to stop the cooking. Blot the corn with paper towels to remove all of the water. Place in a large mixing bowl.

Add the diced green and red peppers and the onion to the corn. In a small bowl, combine the Cajun Mayonnaise, sour cream, sugar, and salt. Add to the corn mixture and mix well. Sprinkle the minced tarragon over the salad, gently mix in, and refrigerate until ready to serve. Remove from the refrigerator about 30 minutes before serving.

Serves 6 to 8. Can be easily doubled for a crowd.

RAISIN BREAD PUDDING

I went back in time to my childhood for this recipe. This was an old family favorite, and it must have been 20 years since I made it. The memories have worn well. I've changed the recipe slightly (a little less sugar, a little more bread), but the result is as delicious as ever.

Place the bread cubes in the top of a double boiler. Add the sugar and toss well. Beat the eggs, milk, and vanilla together until well blended. Pour over the bread cubes. Cover and place over a pot of simmering water for 45 minutes. Do not stir!

*I*n the meantime, place the ice cream in the workbowl of a food processor fitted with a metal blade. Add the nuts and Poire William. Process until blended. Put back in the freezer to harden.

Serve the pudding warm with the "doctored" ice cream.

Serves 6.

K.T.

7 ounces good-quality raisin bread, buttered on both sides and cubed

2/3 cup dark brown sugar, firmly packed

3 large eggs

1 cup milk

1 teaspoon pure vanilla extract

. . . .

TOPPING

1 pint good-quality vanilla ice cream (Haagen Daz is always great)

1/4 cup chopped toasted pecans

1 tablespoon Poire William, Calvados, or Applejack

THE WEDDING TABLE

---

*Chili Verde
Empanadas*
•
*New Potatoes
Stuffed with Goat
Cheese*
•
Gravlax
•
Veal Rollatine
•
Lobster Pasta Salad
•
*Confetti Rice Salad
in Tomato Cups*
•
*Mixed Greens with
Edible Flowers*
•
Baby Bagels
•
Walnut Wedding Ring
•
*White on White
Wedding Cake*
•
*Rice Flour Chocolate
Shortbread*

THE WEDDING TABLE

A wedding is the ultimate celebration! It is a celebration of love, of family, the promise of the future, and the link with the past. In many cultures it involves days of dancing and feasting. Even in some of the world's poorest cultures, a father has a great responsibility to give his daughter to her husband in the most lavish manner he can possibly afford. We in America have taken a somewhat more balanced view of this celebration, although many daddies still do dig deeply into their pockets to provide the "perfect" event.

Cake design by Jane Foley

Styles in weddings have definitely changed over the years. When Dan and I were married in 1971 (Gulp!), weddings were small and informal, if they occurred at all. Vows were handwritten and ceremonies took place in some very unlikely but "meaningful" locations.

Today we have returned to more traditional and formal weddings. They frequently have guest lists of 200 to 500. Receptions are held in local hotels or country clubs.

Here the authors propose a menu for a smaller affair. If you enjoy the intimacy of a backyard garden or private home and have a few friends or relatives that like to cook, this would be a delicious and elegant way to have a wedding.

We offer two hors d'oeuvres which can be passed as the guests first arrive or during the receiving line. Georgia has placed a spicy filling in a tasty chive-cream cheese pastry to produce Chili Verde Empanadas. Diane crisp roasts tiny potatoes and then fills them with a tangy goat cheese and pepper bacon filling.

The buffet table holds a wonderful array of colorful foods. The three "main courses" include a beautifully spiraled Veal Rollatine, a Lobster Pasta Salad, and a melt-in-your mouth Gravlax. We have rounded out the menu with two salads - Whole Tomatoes Stuffed with Confetti Rice and Mixed Greens with Edible Flowers Salad - and two delicious breads - homemade Baby Bagels and a savory Walnut Wedding Ring.

Dessert must include a lovely wedding cake. Although the cake in our photograph was decorated by a true artist, Jane Foley, we feel that a passionate amateur baker could attempt it. The cake is delicious and wedding white. But my palate always yearns for something chocolate at dessert time. Thus I have included some miniature Rice Flour Chocolate Shortbread cookies to act as tiny groom's cakes.

The menu works very well with a sparkling wine from start to finish. Your budget will dictate the label. There are some very fine, crisp, and inexpensive sparkling wines from Spain. Freixenet is a label we recommend. In the mid-price range, Dan and I have long favored Korbel Naturel, a fine, California sparkling wine. If the budget is in great shape, partake of the world's finest – a true French champagne such as Tattinger, Moet et Chandon, or Dom Perignon. Perrier or plain club soda with lime is perfectly fine for the nondrinker. A tasty punch is also an alternative if time allows, but, please, not too sweet.

When researching and developing this menu we were very concerned about its "do-ahead-ability." Here is a brief guide. The empanadas and both breads can be baked a couple of weeks in advance and frozen. The cake layers and cookies can also be done at this time and frozen. A couple of hours before serving, refresh the breads and the empanadas in a 325 degree oven for about 10 minutes.

The Gravlax must be started on its cure a week before the event, but this is virtually all that needs to be done to it. The Veal Rollatines can be assembled and baked two or three days before serving.

The day before the wedding you can make the filling for the potatoes and the dressing for the Mixed Greens with Edible Flowers. The greens for the salad can be cleaned at this *time and wrapped in kitchen towels in the refrigerator. The Lobster Pasta Salad can also be made at this point and is in fact better given a day for the flavors to meld. This is also the time to finish frosting and decorating the cake.*

What remains for serving day includes roasting and filling the potatoes. This is also the time to mix the rice salad and hollow out the tomatoes. It is best not to fill the tomatoes until about an hour before serving. Toss the Mixed Greens with Edible Flowers and slice the Veal Rollatine and the Gravlax just before serving.

Decorations for the food tables are dependent on time, imagination, and budget, but lots of fresh flowers are a must. Find a friend who perhaps is not so skilled in the kitchen to arrange them. Just remember to provide the colors of the season and reflect the style of the setting.

Kathleen Taggart

CHILI VERDE EMPANADAS

With the metal blade in place in a food processor, blend the butter and cream cheeses. Put the flour and salt evenly over the top of the mixture and process by pulsing until the dough just begins to pull together. Remove and wrap in plastic wrap and refrigerate for several hours before rolling out. This dough can also be frozen for later use.

Roast the peppers by burning the skin over a flame or under the broiler until they are black and blistered. Place in a plastic bag and put in the refrigerator for 10 minutes. Remove and scrape off the skins, removing seeds and ends. Chop the peppers fine.

In a heavy skillet, cook the pork over medium high heat until you have rendered out any fat and the meat loses its red color. Add the garlic and onion, and brown with the meat. Add the peppers, salt, and tomatoes. Cook over medium heat about 30 minutes. Set aside to cool to room temperature. In the food processor with the metal blade, process this mixture until well blended and no large chunks of meat remain.

Take one fourth of the pastry and roll it out to about 1/8 inch thickness. Cut the pastry into 3-inch circles with a cookie cutter. (I use a scalloped edge cutter.) Place a generous 2 teaspoons of filling near the center of the bottom half of each circle. With your finger, wet the outside edge of half of the circle with water so it will seal. Fold the other half over to make a half-moon shape. Crimp the edges well with a fork. Place on a nonstick cookie sheet or one lined with parchment paper.

Beat the egg lightly and brush on top of each empanada with a small pastry brush. Be careful not to get egg on the cookie sheet. Continue with the remaining pastry and filling.

Bake at 375 to 400 degrees for 20 to 25 minutes until well browned. As soon as you remove them from the oven, sprinkle just a little of the sugar on top. Serve hot or at room temperature.

These empanadas can be made ahead and frozen unbaked. They will take a little longer to bake. Brush with the egg glaze before baking not before freezing.

Makes about 100 hors d'oeurves.

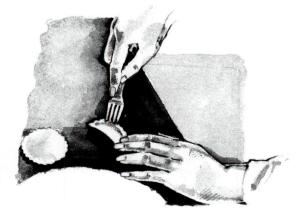

CREAM CHEESE PASTRY
1 pound (4 sticks) unsalted butter, room temperature
6 ounces cream cheese, room temperature
6 ounces cream cheese with chives, room temperature
4 cups all-purpose flour
1/2 teaspoon salt

....

CHILI VERDE FILLING
3-4 jalapeño peppers, roasted and peeled
1 Anaheim pepper, roasted and peeled
2 pounds lean ground pork
5 large cloves garlic, minced
1 1/2 large onions, chopped fine
Salt to taste
1 1/2 large ripe tomatoes, peeled and chopped
1 egg
2 tablespoons sugar

50 tiny red potatoes, cleaned

8 slices pepper bacon

3 (5 1/2-ounce) packages goat cheese

· · · · · · · · · · · · · · · · ·

Pastry bag and #6 star tip

NEW POTATOES STUFFED WITH GOAT CHEESE

Try to buy tiny red potatoes (called creamers) about 1 1/2-inches in diameter. They are a perfect hors d'oeuvre size. The goat cheese I use for this recipe comes in 5 1/2-ounce plastic packages and is made by S.A. Couturier from France. When blended in the food processor this particular goat cheese becomes creamy yet holds its shape for piping through a pastry tube.

Preheat the oven to 350 degrees. Place the potatoes on a baking sheet, pierce two holes in each potato, then roast uncovered for 1 1/2 hours. Remove from the oven and let cool for 30 minutes.

*I*n the meantime, cook the bacon until crisp, let cool, then mince very finely. (If the pieces of bacon are too large they will get stuck in the pastry tip.)

*P*lace the goat cheese in the workbowl of a food processor and process until smooth. Add the finely minced bacon, process 30 seconds more, then remove. Fill a pastry bag that has been fitted with a #6 star tip with the goat cheese mixture. (This can be done a day ahead.) Refrigerate until needed. Remove from the refrigerator one hour before serving.

Cut the potatoes in half. Using a small melon baller, scoop a small bit of potato from each potato half. Pipe a rosette of the goat cheese mixture onto each potato half and serve.

NOTE: The potatoes should be roasted the morning of the wedding then left at room temperature. If you refrigerate the roasted potatoes the skins will shrivel.

Makes 100 hors d'oeuvres.

DM

GRAVLAX

One of the purest, least embellished of salmon preparations, gravlax is a Scandinavian specialty in which the fish is cured by means of a salt and sugar rub. No cooking is involved. It is the next closest thing, I believe, to Japanese "sashimi," or raw fish. Frequently gravlax is seasoned with fresh dill, and black or white cracked pepper and occasionally a brandy like cognac. Spruce sprigs are often called for, too. Lacking a handy spruce tree, I have included gin in my recipe so that its mild juniper berry flavor accents the seasoning mix. I've called for a hefty portion of salmon here in order to feed a wedding crowd.

Scale and fillet the salmon (or have it done for you), leaving the skin on. Select a glass or ceramic baking dish with 2-inch sides that fits the length of the fish as closely as possible. Place one fillet skin side down in the dish. Rub with half the salt and sugar. Spread the dill over the fish and grind on some pepper. Slowly drizzle the gin over the fish so as to not rinse off all the salt/sugar cure. Rub the other fillet with the remaining salt/sugar cure and arrange it skin side *up* so that its widest end rests on top of the lower fillet's narrowest part.

Place a sheet of plastic wrap over the fish. Select an identical baking dish or some other large, flat object to rest on top of the fish. Place something that weighs several pounds in the top dish. I use cans of food or full beer bottles. Place the weighted salmon in the refrigerator for 5 days, turning it after 2 or 3 days.

To serve, skin the fillets. Carve into 1/4-inch slices. Arrange on a platter garnished with fresh dill or parsley. Gravlax will remain good for several days if it is kept cold. It may be frozen. It may also be grilled as if it were a fresh piece of fish.

Serves 50 to 75 as part of a buffet table.

1 9-pound center cut chinook (king) salmon
3/4 cup coarse salt
3/4 cup sugar
1 bunch fresh dill, coarsely chopped, or 1/4 cup dried
Several very coarse grinds pepper
1/2 cup gin

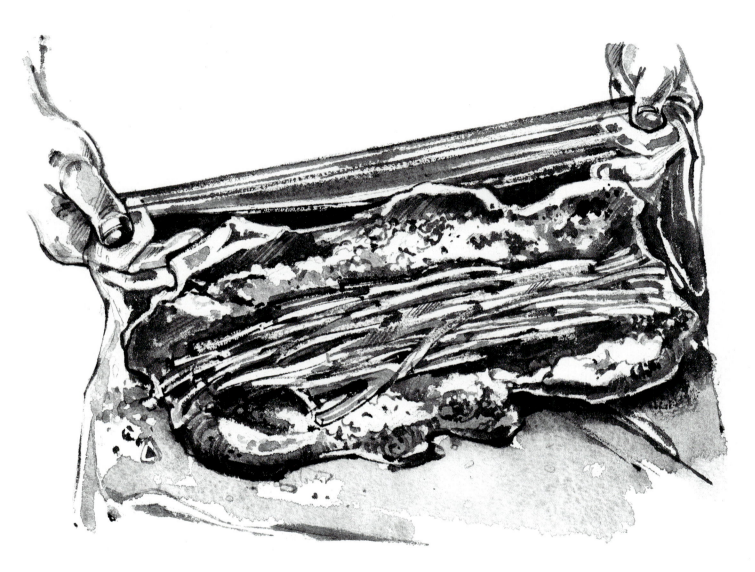

Veal Rollatine

VEAL ROLLATINE

This is a wonderful example of charcuterie (the French term for a cold meat preparation). The inspiration comes from a recipe by Craig Claiborne and Pierre Franey, and they give the original credit to Paula Peck. (Food is often an evolutionary process.) No matter how it came about, this dish looks stunning and is really quite fun to make.

Preheat oven to 350 degrees. Cook the julienned carrots in boiling salted water for 10 minutes. Drain and rinse under cold water. Set aside.

Take two pieces of plastic wrap and overlap them on a counter or worktop. Lay the pieces of veal on the plastic in the form of a rectangle. Lay more plastic wrap over the veal and pound the meat with a smooth-bottomed meat pounder until very thin. You may reposition the meat while you pound to make the rectangle clearer. Remove the top layer of plastic. Cover the pounded veal entirely with the thin-sliced salami.

Mix the bread crumbs, parsley, 4 tablespoons olive oil, and capers. Spread this mixture over the salami. Put the other two tablespoons of olive oil in an 8-inch nonstick skillet. Beat the eggs lightly with a whisk. Heat the olive oil and add the eggs. Sprinkle the crumbled feta cheese on the eggs. Cook the eggs until they are soft scrambled. Set aside to cool slightly.

When the eggs have cooled sufficiently, spoon them over the bottom third of the breadcrumbs. Place the very thinly sliced prosciutto over the eggs. Bunch the julienned carrots down the center of the prosciutto.

Begin rolling the rollatine on the egg side. Use the plastic wrap on the bottom to help roll. Slowly try to wrap the prosciutto around the carrots and continue to roll until completely rolled. Stuff any filling back up inside the rollatine if it slips out while rolling.

Cover the meat lengthwise with the bacon. Tie the meat securely with twine in three places. Place the roll on a roasting rack in a baking pan. Bake 50 minutes.

This may be served warm. It is excellent with a fresh tomato sauce. Otherwise, allow to cool completely and then place in the refrigerator. Serve at room temperature.

Makes 25 to 30 thin slices.

K. T.

---

3 medium carrots, peeled and julienned
12 to 14 ounces veal scallopini
1/4 pound Genoa salami, very thinly sliced
1 1/2 cups fresh bread crumbs
1/2 cup chopped parsley
4 tablespoons olive oil
1 tablespoon capers, rinsed and drained
2 tablespoons olive oil
6 large eggs
2 ounces feta cheese, crumbled
1/4 pound prosciutto, very thinly sliced
3 or 4 slices bacon

COURT BOUILLON
2 quarts water

3 quarter-sized slices fresh ginger

2 carrots, chopped

2 ribs celery, chopped

1 leek, white part only, chopped

2 sprigs fresh thyme

1 bay leaf

8 whole peppercorns

1 teaspoon coarse salt

1/2 cup pale dry sherry

. . . .

VINAIGRETTE
2 cups olive oil

2/3 cup rice wine vinegar

2/3 cup heavy cream

5 teaspoons coarse salt

2 tablespoons sugar

Freshly ground black pepper, to taste

1/4 cup minced fresh tarragon

. . . .

1 whole live lobster, about 1-1/2 pounds

3 pounds #91 orecchiette pasta (by DeCecco, in the blue box)

6 lobster tails, 6-8 ounces each

2 large sweet red peppers

6 ribs celery, peeled

6 tablespoons fresh chives cut into 1/2-inch lengths

LOBSTER PASTA SALAD

The pasta for this salad is called orecchiette, which translates as "little ears," but the shape of this pasta reminds me of workmen's hardhats. The flavors of lobster and fresh tarragon marry (!) beautifully, and the sweet red peppers and celery add color and crunch.

This salad is at its best when made the day before. The court bouillon can be made weeks ahead and frozen.

For the Court Bouillon, combine all the ingredients except the sherry in a large pan. Bring to a boil and simmer for 30 minutes. Strain, discard the vegetables, add the sherry, and cool. Use or freeze until needed, adding enough water to make 2 quarts. After each use freeze again. The Court Bouillon will keep up to 6 months in the freezer.

In a quart jar with a tight fitting lid, combine all of the ingredients for the vinaigrette. Taste and adjust the seasonings, then set aside.

Bring two large pots of water to a boil. Place the live lobster head first into one of the pots of boiling water. Cook it for 8 minutes from the time the water returns to a boil. When the whole lobster is done, remove it from the pot using tongs, and place it under cold running water to stop the cooking. Let it drain well on paper towels.

In the meantime, add 1 tablespoon of salt and 2 tablespoons of oil to the second pot of boiling water and bring back to a boil. Add 2 pounds of the pasta and cook until al dente, about 12 to 15 minutes. Stir occasionally. Drain the pasta in a colander and run under cold water until cold. Spread the pasta out on a clean linen towel to remove any excess water, then place in a very large mixing bowl. Repeat the same process with the other pound of pasta, using the pot of water you cooked the lobster in.

In another large pan bring the Court Bouillon to a boil. Simmer the 6 lobster tails in the Court Bouillon for 8 minutes from the time the water returns to a boil. Remove them from the pot and place under cold running water to stop the cooking. Let drain on paper towels.

Clean the red peppers and remove the seeds. Cut the peppers into 1/2-inch wide strips. Cut the strips to form small triangles, 1/2-inch on each side. Add to the pasta. Do the same for the celery.

Remove the meat from the lobster tails and tear it gently into small pieces using your fingers. Carefully remove the tail meat from the whole lobster, leaving the tail shell intact. Again tear the meat into small pieces. The rest of the lobster meat from the whole lobster should be left in the shell, as the lobster becomes the main garnish for the salad. (Place the lobster on paper towels on a large plate, cover with plastic wrap and refrigerate until serving time.) Add all of the lobster meat to the pasta and toss to combine.

Stir the vinaigrette and add to the pasta, lobster meat, and vegetables. Toss to combine, add the chives, toss again, then cover and refrigerate until 30 minutes before serving.

To serve, use a very large decorative platter, mound the lobster salad on the platter leaving a trough down the center. Place the whole lobster in the center, spreading out its claws and legs.

Serves 50 as part of the wedding buffet.

DM

CONFETTI RICE SALAD IN TOMATO CUPS

Soak the cherries in the sherry for about an hour. Drain, reserving 2 tablespoons of the sherry for the mayonnaise.

Bring the beef broth to a boil in a large pot. Add the rice gradually, stirring with a fork. When the broth returns to a boil, lower the heat and simmer, covered, for about 20 minutes, or until all liquid is absorbed. Remove from the heat, stir once, and spread the rice onto a cookie sheet and let cool to room temperature.

Allow the peas to thaw completely. They will not be cooked. Cook the corn in boiling water for about 3 minutes (just blanch it). Remove and drain. Set aside to cool.

Now make the Sherry Mayonnaise.

When the rice and corn have cooled, mix them with the peas, cherries, and parsley in the large bowl. Add the mayonnaise and then the sour cream, blending well. Add the salt and pepper. Taste and adjust the seasonings. Cover and refrigerate. This part of the salad can, and should, be prepared the day before.

Cut the tops off the tomatoes after you have washed them. With a melon baller or grapefruit spoon, hollow out the tomatoes, discarding the insides. You may want to cut a very thin slice off the bottom so the stuffed tomatoes will sit flat on the plate and not roll sideways.

Before serving time, stuff the tomatoes with the rice salad, filling them to the top. Cut the strips of red pepper into 1/2-inch pieces and garnish the top of the salad. Wash the romaine and separate the leaves. Line a large platter or glass serving plate with the lettuce leaves and arrange the stuffed tomatoes on the leaves.

SHERRY MAYONNAISE

In the workbowl of a food processor fitted with the metal blade, put the eggs and yolk, sherry, salt and pepper. Pulse a few times to mix. With the machine running, *very gradually* add the oil through the feed tube. It must be added in a very slow, thin stream or the mixture will not emulsify.

Serves 50 to 60.

* Dried red tart cherries are available in specialty delis and by mail order from Williams-Sonoma or American Spoon Foods, Inc. in Petoskey, Michigan.

---

1 6-ounce package dried red tart cherries*
1 cup dry sherry or marsala wine
....

6 1/2 cups beef broth or stock (you may use canned broth)
3 cups long-grain white rice
....

2 packages (10 ounces) frozen tiny peas, thawed and drained
1 package (20 ounces) frozen corn
....

1/2 cup minced fresh parsley
Sherry wine mayonnaise (recipe follows)
1 cup sour cream
2 teaspoons salt
1 teaspoon freshly ground white pepper
....

50-60 small salad tomatoes (about 2 inches in diameter)
....

1-2 red peppers, cleaned and cut into very thin strips
2 large heads romaine lettuce, washed and drained
....

SHERRY MAYONNAISE
2 extra large eggs plus 1 yolk
2 tablespoons reserved sherry or marsala wine
1/2 teaspoon salt
1/4 teaspoon ground white pepper
2 cups vegetable oil

2 large heads butter lettuce

3 large heads red leaf lettuce

1 head escarole

4 carrots, peeled and julienned into 1 1/2-inch lengths

1 16-ounce can shoestring beets (not pickled)

. . . .

ORANGE VINAIGRETTE

1 cup extra virgin olive oil

3/4 cup freshly squeezed orange juice

1/4 cup freshly squeezed lemon juice

1 tablespoon coarse salt

1 1/2 teaspoons sugar

Freshly ground black pepper, to taste

1/2 cup finely chopped fresh mint

. . . .

Fresh edible flowers, pansies or nasturtiums, about 20 flowers

MIXED GREENS WITH EDIBLE FLOWERS

Here in the Northwest mixing edible flowers with salads and pasta has become quite popular and rather fanciful. They are readily available from specialty green grocers and make for a lovely, colorful presentation—especially on a wedding buffet.

Wash the lettuces and use a salad spinner to dry them. Wrap them in layers in cotton tea towels, place in plastic bags, and refrigerate. Lettuce prepared this way will keep well for 2 to 3 days.

*P*lace the carrots in a small mixing bowl and reserve. Rinse and drain the beets and reserve in a separate mixing bowl.

*I*n a jar with a tight fitting lid, combine all the ingredients in the vinaigrette. Shake to combine, then taste and adjust the seasonings. Spoon about 1/3 cup of dressing over the carrots and over the beets. Cover and let marinate for 1 to 2 days. Refrigerate the remaining dressing. Let stand at room temperature for one hour before serving.

*T*o serve, line the perimeter of two large, shallow serving bowls with the butter lettuce. Tear the red leaf lettuce, escarole, and remaining butter lettuce into small pieces, toss together in a large mixing bowl, then divide between the two serving bowls. Shake the dressing well, and spoon lightly over one bowl of greens. (You do not want to coat the greens, as they would wilt rapidly on the buffet.) Decoratively spread half of the carrots and beets over the greens, then garnish with half of the edible flowers. When ready for the second bowl of salad, repeat the above steps.

Serves 50 for a buffet.

DM

BABY BAGELS

New York bagels, Philadelphia bagels, Log Angeles bagels – I've heard praises sung for all of them. But nevermind all those because you can make a truly terrific bagel in your own kitchen. It's fun! For our wedding menu I've chosen to make these a bit more petite than usual since they are part of a larger buffet. These bagels don't hold well at all. Freeze them after they have cooled an hour or so, and reheat just before serving.

To make the dough, stir the sugar and yeast into the warm water and allow to sit until foamy, about 5 to 10 minutes. Stir in the salt. Place the flour in the workbowl of a food processor fitted with the dough blade. (If using a stand mixer proceed in your usual breadmaking manner.) With the machine running, slowly pour the yeast mixture into the flour until a dough ball has formed. Allow the dough to rotate (knead) inside the machine for 1 minute, adding flour by the tablespoon if needed to prevent the dough from sticking to the workbowl. Place the dough in a gallon-sized plastic bag, squeeze out all the air, and place a wire twist at the *top* of the bag so that the dough has room to expand. Allow to rise until doubled in size, approximately 45 to 60 minutes, depending upon temperature.

Lay two clean kitchen towels on the counter. Deflate the dough and cut it into 40 equal pieces (a kitchen scale helps to get even portions). Using your hands, roll out each piece of dough into a rope-like shape about six inches long and about as big around as the average fountain pen. As you roll out each piece of dough, wrap it around your index and middle fingers, overlap the ends an inch or so, and firmly squeeze the "joint" you've made. Roll the seam back and forth between your fingers and the palm of your other hand so as to even out the joint a bit. Set your ring of dough on the towel. Continue until all 40 pieces of dough have been transformed into ring shapes.

Bring 3 quarts of water to a boil in a 5-quart pan which has fairly low, straight sides. Add 1 1/2 tablespoons sugar to the water. Preheat the oven to 450 degrees and adjust two shelves to the middle level. Select two heavy baking sheets and either line them with parchment paper or sprinkle them liberally with cornmeal to prevent the bagels from sticking. Don't grease the baking sheets.

When the bagels have risen a bit and are looking slightly "puffy" drop 8 or so into the boiling water. After 15 seconds turn them over to boil another 15 seconds. Using a metal soup skimmer or large, slotted spoon, lift the bagels out of the water and onto the towels again. Continue until all the bagels have been boiled. (If you'd like to know why most bagels have the texture of a rubber eraser just leave the last ring of dough in the water for 5 minutes before baking it!) Place the bagels on the lined baking sheets, brush with the beaten egg white, and bake about 8 minutes. Remove the sheets from the oven, turn the bagels over and return the pans to the oven, reversing their location this time. Bake until the bagels are a beautiful golden brown, approximately about 8 or 9 more minutes. Cool the bagels on a rack and freeze within two or three hours.

Makes 40 miniature bagels.

1 1/2 cups warm water, not over 115 degrees
1/4 teaspoon sugar
1 tablespoon or 1 package active dry yeast
1 teaspoon coarse salt
4 cups bread flour, approximately
1 egg white, beaten

2 cups warm milk, not over 115 degrees

2 tablespoons molasses

1 tablespoon or 1 packet active dry yeast

2 teaspoons coarse salt

1/2 cup walnut oil

3 cups whole wheat flour

1 cup rye or buckwheat flour

2 cups plus 2 tablespoons bread flour, more if needed

1 cup coarsely chopped walnuts

Cornmeal or parchment paper

1 egg, beaten

WALNUT WEDDING RING

Here is a bread that has a nutty, tender taste and is beautiful to look at. Walnut oil adds terrific flavor – look for it at specialty food stores. With six cups of flour in the recipe, you'll need an 8-cup capacity food processor. If your food processor is not that large, cut the recipe in half, make two half batches, and blend them together with your hands; or use a large stand mixer.

I form this into two large, impressive rings. Slice one into serving pieces and arrange attractively around the other (whole) ring in a large flat basket or wicker tray.

Stir the molasses and yeast into the warm milk. Allow to stand until foamy, about 5 minutes. Stir in the salt and walnut oil.

Place the flours (measure by stirring the flours first, then dipping a dry measure cup into the flour and scraping off the excess) in the workbowl of a large capacity food processor fitted with the dough blade. Stir up the yeast mixture and, with the machine running, slowly pour it into the flour mixture. If you hear "sloshing" you are pouring too quickly! Allow a dough ball to form – adding more flour by the tablespoonful if necessary to prevent the dough from sticking to the sides of the bowl – and let the machine run for one minute to knead the dough. Remove the dough, place it in a gallon-sized plastic bag, squeeze out all the air, and place a wire twist at the *top* of the bag so that the dough has room to expand. Allow to rise in a warm place until the dough has doubled in size, approximately 1 to 1 1/2 hours depending on temperature.

Turn the dough out of the bag, flatten it on a counter, and sprinkle with the chopped walnut meats. Press them into the dough, roll the dough up into a log shape, flatten the dough with your clenched fists, roll it into a log again, and repeat twice more to thoroughly incorporate the nuts into the bread. Divide the dough in half, and roll each one to form a log 2 inches in diameter. Now form each log into a large ring loaf. Overlap the ends an inch or so, and firmly squeeze the "joint" you've made. Place each ring loaf on a cookie sheet which has been covered with parchment paper or sprinkled with cornmeal to prevent sticking. There is no need to butter the cookie sheets. Using a very sharp knife or razor blade, cut five slashes, spaced evenly, across the top of each ring. Cover each with a clean kitchen towel and allow to rise until doubled in size, appproximately 30 to 50 minutes.

Preheat the oven to 375 degrees. Brush the beaten egg gently over the surface of the dough using a soft pastry brush. Bake the bread until it registers at least 180 degrees on an instant read thermometer, likely about 25 to 30 minutes. Cool on a rack.

The loaves will freeze well for a month or so if tightly wrapped in plastic and/or foil.

Makes 2 ring loaves.

WHITE ON WHITE WEDDING CAKE

A beautiful wedding cake is easily the focal point of a food table, but is frequently a disappointment to eat. It does not have to be so. I'm providing a recipe here that Dan and I used in our catering days, originally published by Maida Heatter who claims it originated at a hotel in Hawaii. This white cake is flavored with a rich chocolate ganache and raspberry preserves. It's delicious and easy to make.

We employed the help of a talented professional, Jane Foley of Il Dolci bakery, to make our cake for photography. However, this cake is not an impossible challenge for a dedicated amateur. The cake can be baked several weeks before the wedding, tightly wrapped, and frozen. The ganache can easily be made a week ahead. The buttercream can be refrigerated or frozen, then slowly brought back to room temperature before spreading on the cake. Decorations can be kept quite simple: witness the chocolate curls Jane employed as garnish for our cake.

The recipe for the cake that follows is for six times the original recipe. This gives us two 12-inch, two 8-inch, and two 6-inch cakes. Each layer is then split in half. Therefore, each cake tier consists of four layers with alternating fillings of chocolate ganache and seedless raspberry preserves. This cake would feed almost three times our 50 person guest list, but it is definitely more impressive being a little oversized— and the leftovers are great.

I am giving full measurements, but unless you have a professional-sized mixer you will need to divide this recipe into batches as your mixer and oven space allow. Jane strongly advised using bake-even or Magic Cake strips on the 12-inch pans to insure even cooking. Cooking times for the various layers will require a watchful and cautious eye.

CAKE

Sift together the flour, baking powder, and salt. Set aside. With an electric mixer, beat the butter until soft. Add the vanilla and then the sugar. Beat thoroughly, scraping down the sides of the mixing bowl, until the sugar is well incorporated. On low speed gradually add the dry ingredients and the milk in five alternating additions, beating well each time. Beat on high speed for a few seconds. Add the *unbeaten* egg whites and then beat on high speed for 2 minutes. The mixture may look slightly curdled, but that is okay.

Preheat the oven to 350 degrees. Butter each of the baking pans to be used. Cut rounds of parchment for each. Then butter and flour the parchment in the pans. Divide the batter among the various sizes of pans filling each pan 2/3 of the way full. Bake as many pans as will comfortably fit in your oven, allowing air to circulate between the pans. Refrigerate the remaining batter until ready to bake. Begin checking the 6-inch pans after 25 minutes. The 8-inch pans will probably take 30 to 35 minutes, and the 12-inch pans 40 to 50 minutes. Test with a cake tester or toothpick. As soon as either of these reads clean, remove from the oven. Try to remove *before* they start to shrink from the sides of the pan.

When out of the oven, let them stand for 5 minutes. Remove the cake from the pan onto a cooling rack. Clean and reprepare the baking pans immediately if more batter awaits.

GANACHE

This is my favorite recipe for ganache. It comes from the fine French cooking of Anne Willan. I used it for many years as the base for my Chocolate Truffles. Here it alternates

CAKE
- 12 cups all-purpose flour
- 7 tablespoons double-acting baking powder
- 2 tablespoons salt
- 6 sticks (24 ounces) unsalted butter
- 2 tablespoons pure vanilla extract
- 9 cups granulated sugar
- 6 cups milk
- 24 egg whites (may be frozen, and thawed)

GANACHE
24 ounces good-quality semisweet chocolate
(Callebaut is excellent)
2 cups heavy cream
. . . .

EGG WHITE BUTTERCREAM
3/4 cup water
2 cups granulated sugar
1 1/3 cups egg whites
6 tablespoons sugar
12 sticks (3 pounds) unsalted butter, at room
temperature
. . . .

OPTIONAL FLAVORINGS
3 tablespoons clear vanilla, or 1/2 cup clear
liqueur, such as Poire William

with seedless raspberry preserves as the filling for the cake layers. You could certainly use all raspberry or all ganache, but the combination is classic and delicious.

Chop the chocolate. Bring the cream to a boil in a large saucepan. Remove from the heat. Add the chopped chocolate and beat until smooth. Set aside and allow to cool and thicken. Spread a thin layer on top of each layer to be covered with chocolate.

The ganache can be stored in the refrigerator or frozen. It will need to be softened before applying to the cake. A microwave works beautifully for this.

EGG WHITE BUTTERCREAM

This recipe comes to us from a lovely friend and outstanding baker, Mary Donnally. Mary saved me in my hunt for an egg white-based buttercream. For the wedding cake, we found that a buttercream consisting of egg yolks was too yellow. Mary came up with a recipe that produces a lovely buttercream of light ivory color.

Combine the water and 2 cups of sugar in a medium saucepan over moderate heat. Bring to a boil and boil until a candy thermometer reads 238 or 240 degrees. In the meantime, beat the egg whites until foamy. Gradually add the 6 tablespoons of sugar while continuing to beat. Beat until soft peaks form. With the machine running, add the hot sugar syrup in a steady stream. Continue to beat until the mixture cools to room temperature.

It is important that the butter be almost the same texture as the egg white mixture when you add it. Beating at medium speed, add the butter in about 3-tablespoon pieces. If the mixture looks like it might curdle turn the mixer to high and beat vigorously for a minute. When all the butter has been incorporated add optional flavorings.

The buttercream can be made a few weeks in advance and frozen. Defrost gradually in the refrigerator and then bring to room temperature before rebeating.

Makes approximately 12 cups.

TO ASSEMBLE THE CAKE

To assemble the cake split each layer horizontally. You'll now have four layers for each size. Set aside one of the smallest sized layers. Spread one layer with seedless raspberry preserves, the next layer with ganache, and so on until all but the reserved layer (the top) have been spread with either preserves or ganache.

Make or buy a cardboard cake round slightly smaller than each size layer. Place the 12" board on a serving platter and slip wax paper strips all around underneath the cardboard to make cleanup easier after frosting the cake. Dab a tablespoon of ganache on the board, smear it around a little, and gently press a 12" cake layer on the board. Top with the other three 12" layers, alternating the toppings. Stack the 8" layers on their cake circle in the same fashion, then the 6" layers. Cut 12 heavy plastic straws so that their lengths just match the height on the 12" stack. Insert them into the cake in a random fashion to support the other stacks. Do the same with the 8" stack, perhaps using a few less straw pieces. Gently place the 8" stack on the 12" stack, then place the 6" stack on top. Frost the entire cake and decorate as desired. Pull the wax paper strips from around the bottom. The cake is ready to serve.

K. T.

RICE FLOUR CHOCOLATE SHORTBREAD

Shortbread has been one of my favorite cookies ever since I made a buttery James Beard recipe. The inspiration for this shortbread came from a local dessert restaurant. I always thought that their shortbread was unusually smooth and silky in texture. I found out through Audrey Lieberman (co-author of our first book) that this lovely texture came from using rice flour. I have played with the proportions of rice flour to regular flour to come up with this tender version. It is great with or without dipping it in chocolate.

Preheat the oven to 275 degrees. Place all the dry ingredients in the workbowl of a food processor fitted with the metal blade. Pulse once or twice to blend. Cut each stick of butter into 6 to 8 pieces and place over the dry ingredients. Process until the butter is completely blended into the flour. While processing the butter, add the molasses through the feed tube.

*T*urn the dough out into a 10 x 15 jelly roll pan and press it down evenly in the pan. Bake for 50 minutes. Increase the oven to 300 degrees and bake for 10 minutes more. Remove from the oven and let sit for 5 minutes. Cut in the pan while still warm. Using a table knife cut into 1 1/2-inch squares. Allow to cool completely in the pan before removing.

CHOCOLATE GLAZE

Melt the chocolate in the microwave or on the stove in a heavy-bottomed saucepan. Gently stir in the vegetable oil. Dip each cookie halfway down into the warm chocolate so it is covered in chocolate in a triangular shape. Place on wax paper to harden. The chocolate will harden more quickly by placing them in the refrigerator. The cookies freeze well.

Makes 80 cookies.

* Rice flour is available in oriental markets or the oriental section of some grocery stores.

3 cups all-purpose flour
1 cup rice flour *
1/2 cup unsweetened cocoa
1/4 teaspoon salt
3/4 cup granulated sugar
1 pound (4 sticks) unsalted butter
1/2 cup unsulphured dark molasses

CHOCOLATE GLAZE
1/2 pound semisweet chocolate
1 tablespoon plain vegetable oil

FRIED OYSTER SPINACH SALAD

Blend the Tarragon Mayonnaise with the yogurt, Tabasco, black pepper, and salt and set aside.

In a large salad bowl combine the spinach and vegetables, then set aside.

Drain the oysters and dry well on paper towels. Beat the eggs with the evaporated milk, Tabasco, and black pepper in a wide bowl. Place flour and bread crumbs, separately, in wide, shallow bowls.

Bring oil for deep frying (at least two inches deep) to 375 degrees in a heavy pan. While the oil is heating, toss the spinach and vegetables with the dressing and divide among six large dinner plates. Set aside while frying the oysters. Dust the oysters with the flour, dip into the egg mixture and finally into the breadcrumbs. Deepfry about six at a time maintaining the oil temperature carefully. Fry the oysters for 1 1/2 to 2 minutes per batch or until deep, golden brown. Drain well on paper towels and keep warm in a low oven (175 degrees) while frying the rest of the oysters. When all the oysters are fried, divide them among the salad plates and serve immediately.

Serves 6.

K. T.

HOMEMADE TARRAGON MAYONNAISE

Place the egg in the workbowl of a food processor (or blender) fitted with a metal blade. Add the rest of the ingredients except the oils. Blend for 30 seconds. With the machine running, pour the vegetable oil and olive oil very slowly through the feed tube. Continue until all the oil is used and an emulsion is formed.

K. T.

DRESSING
1 cup homemade Tarragon Mayonnaise (recipe follows) or bottled mayonnaise flavored with 1/4 cup finely chopped fresh tarragon
1/4 cup plain yogurt
1/2 teaspoon Tabasco
1/2 teaspoon freshly ground black pepper
Coarse salt, to taste
....

1 1/2 pounds fresh spinach, cleaned and stemmed
1 medium cucumber (12 ounces), peeled, seeded, and chopped
1 small onion, thinly sliced
1 sweet yellow pepper, julienned
....

30 medium fresh oysters
2 eggs
1/2 cup evaporated milk
1/4 teaspoon Tabasco
1/4 teaspoon freshly ground black pepper
1 cup all-purpose flour
1 1/2 cups dry unflavored bread crumbs
....

Oil for deep frying

1 whole egg
1 tablespoon rice wine vinegar or fresh lemon juice
1 rounded tablespoon Dijon mustard
1/2 cup loosely packed fresh tarragon leaves
1 teaspoon coarse salt
1/2 teaspoon freshly ground black pepper
1 teaspoon sugar
1 cup vegetable oil
1/2 cup extra virgin olive oil

1/2 teaspoon sugar

1 tablespoon or 1 package active dry yeast

1 cup warm water, about 105 degrees

1/4 cup good quality olive oil

1 teaspoon coarse salt

2 1/4 cups all-purpose flour

3/4 cup whole wheat flour

. . . .

2 cloves garlic, peeled and coarsely chopped

4 fresh sage leaves, coarsely chopped

4 to 6-inch sprig fresh rosemary, coarsely chopped

About 1/4 teaspoon coarse salt

2 tablespoons fine quality grated dry cheese, such as parmigiano-reggiano

3 tablespoons good quality olive oil

. . . .

Cornmeal for coating skillet

SUMMER FOCACCIA

Focaccia—sometimes spelled "fugasa"—is a yeast bread rolled into a thin circle and baked on a baking sheet or in a skillet. It comes out looking a lot like a pizza minus the toppings! Don't fear loss of flavor, however; various and sundry herbs and cheeses—not to mention coarse salt and good olive oil—make for very fine eating!

Stir the sugar and yeast into the warm water and allow to stand until foamy. If you are using a mixer, fit the machine with the dough hook, and place the liquid mixture in the bowl. Add the 1/4 cup of olive oil and the 1 teaspoon salt. With the machine running add the flour, a bit at a time, until the dough has gathered together and cleans the sides of the bowl. This may take 4 to 8 minutes or so.

*I*f you are using a food processor, place the flours in the workbowl fitted with the dough blade if the machine has one. Stir the 1 teaspoon salt into the liquid mixture and pour in the 1/4 cup of olive oil. With the machine running, slowly pour the liquids into the workbowl. If you hear a "sloshing" sound you are pouring too fast. When the dough has gathered into a ball and begins rotating inside the machine, allow the processor to run for 45 more seconds.

*P*lace the dough in a gallon-size plastic bag, squeeze out all the air and place a wire twist at the top of the bag so that the dough has room to expand. Or use any other rising method and materials you like! Allow the dough to double in bulk; this could take 30 minutes or well over an hour depending on how warm the room is.

*P*reheat the oven to 425 degrees.

*D*eflate the dough and roll into a circle which will fit in a 12-inch skillet. Sprinkle the skillet well with cornmeal and place the dough circle in it. Cover the dough with a kitchen towel and allow it to rise about 20 minutes. Dimple the dough all over the surface using your first two fingers. Mix the garlic and herbs and sprinkle over the dough. Sprinkle on the 1/4 teaspoon or so of coarse salt and the 2 tablespoons grated cheese. Drizzle the 3 additional tablespoons of olive oil over the top.

*P*lace the pan in the preheated oven and bake until the bread is golden brown, about 20 to 25 minutes. Remove from the pan and cool on a rack. The bread will freeze and reheat nicely if tightly wrapped before freezing.

Serves 6 to 8.

PEACH SLUSH SORBET

The inspiration for this sorbet comes from a delicious drink called "Fuzzy Navel," which is a mixture of orange juice and Peach Schnapps. It is a delightful and very refreshing dessert.

If the peaches are very ripe and sweet, you may wish to alter the amount of sugar or eliminate it altogether. I use superfine sugar because it dissolves better than granulated sugar, especially in an unheated mixture. However, if you cannot find superfine sugar, then use regular sugar, and dissolve it in one cup of the orange juice, add that to the peaches, and proceed with the recipe as given. You can also use frozen peaches, if fresh are not available, but canned peaches will not have the same flavor.

Peel and pit the peaches and cut into thick slices. Process the peaches, sugar, and lemon juice in a food processor or blender until puréed. You can adjust the texture to be as coarse or fine as you desire. I personally like it best when it is medium coarse.

Pour the peach mixture into a bowl and add the Schnapps. Refrigerate until you are ready to make the sorbet. It can even sit overnight. Put the peach mixture and orange juice into an ice cream maker and freeze according to the instructions for the machine you are using. If you do not have an ice cream maker, you can freeze the mixture in ice cube trays and process until fluffy in a food processor when you are ready to serve.

Makes about 1 1/2 quarts.

6 large, ripe peaches (enough to make 4 cups of purée)
1/4 cup superfine sugar
1 tablespoon lemon juice
1/4 cup Peach Schnapps
2 cups orange juice

CHOCOLATE COCONUT BISCOTTI

Preheat oven to 375 degrees. Cover a large cookie sheet with parchment paper. Cream the butter and brown sugar together in a food processor or with a hand mixer. Add egg yolks, one at a time, and then the coconut and vanilla extracts. Mix well after each addition. Add the salt and sifted flour and mix until dough holds together.

Place the dough on a floured surface. Form into a log about two inches in diameter. Cut at approximately 1/4 inch-intervals. Roll each piece into a little log about four inches long. Then form each log into an "S" shape and place on the parchment-lined cookie sheet.

Bake the cookies for approximately 15 minutes or until lightly browned around the edges. Remove to a cooling rack.

While the cookies are cooling, melt the chocolate either in a double boiler or in a microwave. Place a sheet of wax paper on a work surface. When the cookies have cooled, dip one end, about half way up, in the melted chocolate and place on the wax paper. Sprinkle generously with shredded coconut. It may be necessary to rewarm the chocolate once or twice during the process to keep it flowing smoothly. Continue with the remaining cookies. Let the cookies set while the chocolate is hardening. You may place them in the refrigerator to speed this process.

Makes approximately 16 cookies.

K. T.

1/2 stick (2 ounces) unsalted butter
1/2 cup light brown sugar
2 egg yolks
1 teaspoon coconut extract
1/2 teaspoon vanilla extract
1/2 teaspoon salt
1 1/2 cups sifted cake flour
. . . .
4 ounces semisweet chocolate
3 ounces shredded coconut

ARRIVADERCI SUMMER

**Basil Tossed Salad
with Salami**
•
**Smoked Cheese
Lasagne
with Quick Tomato
Sauce**
•
Red Pepper Mélange
•
Peach Tart

*T*here is a tinge of crisp air on your cheek. The days are brilliant, bright, and sunny. You are just beginning to see a hint of color in the trees. You suddenly have this irresistible urge to build a fire! You also have an irresistible urge to start cooking, and eating, some heartier foods. Satisfy this urge and invite a few friends for a hearty and happy meal.

Our casual supper begins with an excellent Basil Tossed Salad With Salami from Georgia. A mixture of fine Mortadella and hard Italian salami in a well-spiced vinaigrette makes this a hearty first course. I follow with a vegetarian entrée. But don't worry, it is no lightweight. Lasagne is an American favorite, and my version, Smoked Cheese Lasagne, is a crowd-pleaser.

We finish out our meal by employing the last of summer's bounty. Dan accompanies the lasagne with a savory Red Pepper Mélange. Dessert is Diane's. She takes the last of the season's golden peaches to make a glowing Peach Tart.

This is a great meal to do for company, as much of it can be prepared in advance. The lasagne can be made a few days ahead of time, fully baked, and then reheated at serving time. It also freezes well, so it can be made weeks before any event. All of the salad ingredients can be pre-cut and the dressing made early in the morning. Toss the salad an hour or so before serving and allow flavors to marry. The red pepper mélange reheats beautifully and is also very good served at room temperature. Finishing the tart is the only last

Kathleen Taggart

DRESSING

1/2 cup olive oil

2 tablespoons lemon juice

2 tablespoons white wine vinegar

1/2 teaspoon dry mustard

1/4 teaspoon ground cinnamon

Coarse salt and freshly ground black pepper, to taste

Pinch sugar

....

1 head romaine lettuce

1 head butter or red leaf lettuce

2 Belgian endive

10-12 basil leaves

2 ounces hard Italian salami, sliced

2 ounces Mortadella (Italian bologna), sliced

1 small bunch red radishes

BASIL TOSSED SALAD WITH SALAMI

Whisk dressing ingredients together and set aside. Wash lettuces and endive well and dry in a salad spinner or with paper towels. Wash and dry basil leaves.

Cut salami and Mortadella into matchstick-sized julienne strips. Set aside.

Clean radishes and trim ends. Cut into very fine julienne strips. (I use the 3x3 mm julienne blade of my food processor.)

Tear lettuce into bite-sized pieces. Cut endive into about 1/4-inch slices and add to lettuces. Mix with half the dressing, tossing well. Add meat strips and toss again. Tear basil leaves in half if they are large, or add smaller ones whole. Add more dressing as needed, don't use it all if salad doesn't need it.

Serve in a bowl garnished with radishes in the center. If using individual salad plates, garnish with radishes.

Serves 8.

SMOKED CHEESE LASAGNE

Melt the butter in a large heavy-bottomed saucepan over medium-low heat. When just beginning to bubble, add the flour. Cook the butter-flour mixture until it *just* begins to turn brown and smells "toasty." While the butter-flour mixture, or roux, is cooking, warm the milk in the microwave or in a small saucepan. Add to the roux, whisking vigorously. Continue to stir until the mixture thickens. Add the salt and nutmeg. Then add all of the shredded cheese. Continue to stir until the mozzarella has almost entirely melted into the sauce. It will thicken it somewhat. The bechamel can be made to this point a day or two in advance and refrigerated. (*Note: If you make the bechamel in advance, rewarm it gently over low heat and add 1/2-cup of the reserved, strained porcini soaking liquid, before assembling the lasagne.)

Heat the first 2 tablespoons of olive oil in a heavy skillet over medium-high heat. When the oil is hot add the onions. Stir briskly. Turn the heat down to medium-low and continue to slowly cook the onions, uncovered for about 30 minutes until "sweet." Season with the salt and pepper and the rosemary and set aside.

While the onions are cooking, cover the dried porcini mushrooms with 1 cup of hot water. Allow to soak for approximately 30 minutes. Pour the porcini juice through a very fine strainer and set aside. Rinse the porcini under the faucet to remove all traces of sand. Dry with a paper towel and chop finely. Set aside.

Heat the second 2 tablespoons of olive oil in another heavy skillet over high heat. Add the sliced fresh mushrooms and sauté briskly for a few minutes until all the moisture has evaporated. Add the chopped porcini and 1/2 teaspoon salt and set aside.

If your fresh lasagne noodles are covered with rice flour, rinse gently under tap water. You may use dried lasagne noodles. Cook according to package directions; drain and rinse. Fresh noodles allow you to skip the cooking step.

Oil a 9x13 lasagne pan or other baking dish. Cover the bottom with a layer of lasagne noodles. Top this with half of the onion mixture. Over this spread about 1/5 of the bechamel and then top with about 1/5 of the grated Caciocavallo. Place another layer of lasagne noodles on top and then repeat the procedure this time using 1/2 of the mushroom mixture. Continue to alternate the layers in the same manner finishing with a layer of lasagne noodles, bechamel, and grated smoked cheese.

Place in a preheated 400 degree oven and bake for 20 minutes. If not nicely browned on top, place under the broiler for a minute or two until well-browned. Let rest for 15 minutes before serving. Top each piece of lasagne with Quick Tomato Sauce.

Serves 6.

K. T.

BECHAMEL
4 tablespoons unsalted butter
5 tablespoons flour
3 cups milk
1/2 teaspoon salt
1/2 teaspoon freshly ground nutmeg
5 ounces smoked mozzarella cheese, shredded
1/2 cup strained porcini soaking liquid *(see * Note)*
....

LASAGNE
2 tablespoons olive oil
1 1/2 pounds yellow onions, sliced thin (2mm food processor blade)
Coarse salt and freshly ground black pepper, to taste
1 tablespoon chopped fresh rosemary
....

1 ounce dried porcini mushrooms
2 tablespoons olive oil
1 pound fresh mushrooms, cleaned and sliced
1/2 teaspoon coarse salt
....

1 pound fresh egg lasagne noodles
7 ounces smoked Caciocavallo cheese, or other good quality smoked cheese, grated

QUICK TOMATO SAUCE

3 tablespoons olive oil
4 cloves garlic
1 large onion
2 28-ounce cans whole tomatoes
6 anchovy fillets, chopped
1/2 cup parsley, chopped
Coarse salt and freshly ground black pepper,
to taste

Heat the olive oil in a heavy skillet over medium-high heat. Chop the garlic and the onion fine. When the oil is hot add the garlic and onion to the pan and cook, stirring regularly until the onion becomes translucent. Add the two cans of tomatoes. Bring the mixture to a boil and then reduce heat to a simmer. Simmer the mixture for 15 minutes stirring occasionally and crushing the whole tomatoes with the back of a wooden spoon.

When mixture has simmered, add the chopped anchovies, parsley, salt, and pepper. Remove from heat.

K. T.

RED PEPPER MÉLANGE

3 tablespoons olive oil
4 large red bell peppers, seeded and sliced in 1/4-inch rings
1 large green bell pepper, seeded and cut in 1/4-inch rings
1 large sweet onion, peeled and sliced in 1/4-inch rings
Coarse salt and freshly ground black pepper, to taste
1/2 teaspoon sugar
2 tablespoons sherry vinegar

I love peppers! Green ones, yellow ones, hot ones, sweet ones — they're all wonderfully loaded with flavor I crave. At the time of this writing red bell peppers—sweet and crimson—are fetching an eye opening $5.99 per pound in most markets. But in the late summer and early fall they can usually be had for a lot less, sometimes even 5 for $1.00! That is when I fill a small sack with them and find excuses to use them in every meal except breakfast, and sometimes even then! Here's such an excuse!

About 20 minutes before serving time heat a large, heavy sauté pan. Add the oil, swirling it around the pan. Toss in the peppers and onion. Cover the pan for 5 minutes and cook over medium heat to soften the vegetables a bit. Uncover the pan, raise the heat to medium-high and cook the mixture, stirring almost constantly, until the peppers have begun to brown and any liquid in the pan has evaporated. Season with salt and pepper, and toss in the sugar and vinegar. Stir well and taste for seasoning. Adjust to your taste with more salt, sugar, or vinegar. Serve hot.

PEACH TART

This tart is best eaten the day it is made. To ease last minute preparations, I prepare the tart shell and the filling the day before I plan to serve them. Then assembling the tart and baking it the day of the party is easy.

In the bowl of a mixer which has a pastry paddle, place the flour, salt, butter, lard, and powdered sugar. With the mixer on a slow speed, combine the flour mixture until the butter is the size of peas. In a small bowl combine the egg yolks, vinegar, vanilla, and sour cream. With the mixer running, add the egg yolk mixture, then quickly add just enough ice water to bind the dough. There should still be separate hunks of dough in the mixer, but by patting the dough together with your hands it should form a ball. Scrape the bowl clean, then you can use the same mixer bowl to make the filling.

Lightly flour a work surface and rolling pin, then roll out the dough into a circle just larger than the tart pan. Fit the dough into the pan, crimp the edges, then refrigerate at least 30 minutes.

To make the filling, cream the butter and sugar. Add the egg yolk and mix, then add the whole egg and cream. Mix thoroughly. Combine the pecans and flour and add to the butter mixture, then add the bourbon. (The filling can be made ahead and refrigerated. Allow to stand at room temperature about 20 to 30 minutes before spreading onto the the prepared pastry dough.)

Preheat the oven to 400 degrees.

To assemble, spread the filling mixture evenly over the bottom of the tart shell. Peel the peaches, cut in halves, remove the pits and cut thin slices. Arrange the peach slices in overlapping concentric circles, beginning along the outside edge. Brush the slices gently with the bourbon. Bake for 30 minutes on the lowest shelf of the oven. Remove and brush with the apple jelly. Bake an additional 10 minutes. Sprinkle with the sugar and bake 5 minutes longer, or until browned. Increase heat if necessary.

Serves 8 to 10.

DM

PASTRY DOUGH
2 cups sifted all-purpose flour
1/4 teaspoon salt
1/4 pound unsalted butter, chilled, cut into eighths
2 tablespoons lard
2 tablespoons powdered sugar
2 egg yolks
1 teaspoon white vinegar
1/2 teaspoon vanilla
1 tablespoon sour cream
1-2 tablespoons ice water

....

FILLING
1/4 pound unsalted butter, room temperature
1/2 cup sugar
1 egg yolk
1 whole egg
1 tablespoon whipping cream
3/4 cup ground pecans
1 tablespoon all-purpose flour
3 tablespoons bourbon

....

3-4 firm, ripe peaches
1 tablespoon bourbon
2 tablespoons apple jelly, melted
1 tablespoon sugar

....

9 to 10-inch tart pan with a removable bottom

FALL SALMON RUN

Here in Oregon, and the Pacific Northwest, we enjoy fresh salmon all year round. On those rare occasions when fresh salmon is unavailable, frozen salmon can always be found.

Salad with Yogurt Dressing
•
Baked Whole Salmon with Rice Stuffing
•
Steamed Broccoli*
•
Dark Honey Ice Cream
•
Crisp Chocolate Pecan Cookies

We present here an elegant, simple menu for a small group of guests (6 to 8 people). A Baked Whole Salmon with Rice Stuffing that includes lots of parsley, cashews, and Middle Eastern spices, is cooked in wine. Dan adds a delightful Salad With Yogurt Dressing that includes chunks of cucumber, green pepper, onion, and mushrooms.

Kathleen's contribution is a Dark Honey Ice Cream made with the darkest honey she could find!! The Crisp Chocolate Pecan Cookies that Diane made are the perfect finishing touch.

We suggest serving a California Chardonnay or a German Moselle to accompany the salmon. Your guests will enjoy the food, and you will have the time to enjoy your guests!!

* Recipe not included.

Georgia M. Vareldzis

DRESSING

3 tablespoons vegetable oil

1 1/2 teaspoons black mustard seed

1/2 teaspoon ground coriander seed

1/2 teaspoon ground cumin

1 1/2 cups plain yogurt

1 tablespoon sherry vinegar

1 tablespoon sugar

Few grinds black pepper

1/4 teaspoon Tabasco sauce or

other brand to taste

Coarse salt, to taste

. . . .

1 cucumber, peeled, seeded and cut into

1-inch pieces

8 ounces mushrooms, cut about the same

size as the cucumbers

1 green pepper, seeded, cut into

1-inch pieces

1 small red onion, peeled, cut into

1-inch pieces, layers separated

Optional: 1 cup cooked potato, cut into

1-inch pieces

Coarse salt and freshly ground black pepper,

to taste

Leaf or romaine lettuce

SALAD WITH YOGURT DRESSING

To make the dressing, heat the oil in a small, heavy skillet along with the mustard seed. Allow the oil and seeds to cook over medium heat (covered with a spatter screen, ideally) until the seeds pop and snap. This releases the wonderful aroma and flavor of the mustard seed. Turn off the heat and allow the pan to cool for a minute or two. Then stir in the coriander and cumin.

*I*n a small mixing bowl combine the yogurt, vinegar, sugar, pepper, Tabasco, and salt. Add the oil-seed mixture and blend thoroughly. Taste for seasoning and correct if necessary.

*T*o make the salad, place the vegetables in a large bowl and toss together. Add enough of the dressing to moisten well. Taste and add more salt or pepper if necessary. Place a leaf of lettuce on each salad plate and top with some of the salad.

Serves 6 to 8.

BAKED WHOLE SALMON WITH RICE STUFFING

Wash the salmon well inside and out. Scrape off any scales on the outside of the fish so that you can use the "juice" from baking the fish on the fish and stuffing. Even though the skin will be discarded, the scales could get into the baking juice.

Squeeze lemon juice inside the fish cavity and set aside.

Heat the olive oil in a large skillet or sauté pan. Sauté the leek, celery, carrot, and nuts over medium heat until tender, about 5 to 10 minutes. Add the rice and stir to coat with oil until it glistens. Add the clam broth, parsley, baharat, and salt. Cook over low heat, stirring occasionally, until all liquid is absorbed. Remove from the heat and allow to cool to room temperature. Never put hot stuffing in cold fish or any meat.

Line a 10x15 inch pan or baking dish with foil and place the salmon in it. Put the cooled stuffing inside the cavity, filling well but not overfull. Any extra stuffing can be baked in a casserole at the same time as the fish. Close the cavity as you would a stuffed turkey, wrapping kitchen twine about skewers placed about 1 inch apart. Pour white wine over the fish. Cover with foil and bake at 375 to 400 degrees for about 30 minutes. Uncover and finish baking. The fish is done when the center bone pulls away from the meat when touched. A general rule of thumb is ten minutes per inch of thickness. Also, when a metal skewer inserted behind the gills meets no resistance, the fish is cooked.

Serve in the baking dish or on a large platter, peeling away and discarding the skin.

Serves 6 to 8.

1 whole salmon, 4-6 pounds
Juice of 1 lemon
. . . .

3-4 tablespoons olive oil
1 leek, thinly sliced
1 stalk celery with leaves, finely chopped
1 carrot, finely chopped
1/2 cup raw cashews, chopped
1 cup long grain white rice
2 cups clam or chicken broth
1 cup fresh parsley, minced
2 teaspoons baharat (recipe follows)
1 teaspoon coarse salt
. . . .

1/2 cup dry white wine
. . . .

BAHARAT: (Middle Eastern spice)
1 tablespoon ground black pepper
1/2 tablespoon ground coriander
1/2 tablespoon ground cloves
1 tablespoon ground cumin
1/4 teaspoon ground cardamom
1/2 teaspoon ground nutmeg
Pinch of ground cinnamon
. . . .

Mix and store in an airtight jar

2 cups half and half

4 egg yolks

1/3 cup *dark* honey (the darker you can find, the more pronounced the flavor will be)

Pinch salt

DARK HONEY ICE CREAM

Heat the half and half in a heavy-bottomed saucepan until just below a boil. In the meantime, beat the egg yolks and honey briefly. Whisking constantly, pour the hot half and half into the egg mixture and then pour all back into the saucepan. Over low heat continue to stir, bringing the custard mixture to 170 degrees on an instant read thermometer. Turn off the heat and continue to stir for a minute or two. Add the pinch of salt. Allow to cool completely and then refrigerate overnight. Freeze in an ice cream maker according to manufacturer's directions.

Makes 1 quart.

K. T.

CRISP CHOCOLATE PECAN COOKIES

Using a mixer, cream the butter and sugar together until fluffy. Add the vanilla and blend. Combine the flour and salt and mix with the butter mixture. Now add the milk and mix. Using a rubber spatula, stir in the chocolate chips and pecans until evenly distributed. Chill the dough for 30 minutes.

Preheat the oven to 400 degrees. Drop the dough by rounded teaspoonfuls, at least 2 inches apart, onto non-stick or well-greased cookie sheets. Bake 8 to 10 minutes, or until lightly browned at the edges. Remove from the oven and let stand about one minute before carefully removing to a cooling rack.

Makes 4 to 5 dozen cookies.

DM

1/4 pound unsalted butter, at room temperature
1/2 cup sugar
1/2 teaspoon vanilla
3/4 cup all-purpose flour
1/4 teaspoon salt
3 teaspoons milk
1/3 cup mini semisweet chocolate chips
1/3 cup *finely* chopped pecans

AN AUTUMN DINNER FOR SPECIAL FRIENDS

Three-Mushroom Sauté with Caraway Crisps

•

Fillet of Sole with Saffron Beurre Blanc

•

Steamed Green Beans*

•

Romaine and Endive Vinaigrette*

•

Apple, Almond and Raisin Tart

By the time September and October roll around, the vacations are over, the children are back in school, and the leaves are beginning to turn. It's then that I start thinking about more formal entertaining. I love to set a complete table, with its battery of forks and spoons and fine china. With that, for me, is the hope of a leisurely-paced dinner and lingering conversations.

This meal begins with some of the colors and treasures of fall...Three Mushroom Sauté with Caraway Crisps. Although it's rather romantic to think about foraging for wild mushrooms in the woods, specialty markets and mushroom growers have practically brought these treasures to our doorsteps. In my favorite stores here, I can usually find fresh shiitake and oyster mushrooms. And when fresh mushrooms are not available, dried shiitake or porcini mushrooms make fine substitutes.

The first course is followed by Fillet of Sole with Saffron Beurre Blanc. Dan created this recipe using petrale sole, though other types of sole would work just as well. The cream-colored fish on a china plate with the saffron-colored sauce is a picture of perfection. To accompany the entrée we suggest some simple steamed or sautéed green beans.

Follow the fish with a salad of your choosing. I suggest tossed greens with some spicy, curly endive or arugula. Our first book, ENTERTAINING PEOPLE, has some wonderful salad recipes to choose from.

When I created this Apple, Almond and Raisin Tart, I was thinking about some of the wonderful flavors that I enjoy with baked apples—raisins, almonds and cinnamon. I've included them all in this recipe and thrown in some Calvados for fun.

To accompany this meal, a blush wine with some character would work especially well with the mushroom sauté. The 1988 De Loach White Zinfandel, which I recently tasted, was very nice. For the sole fillets I would turn to a light, bone dry, yet deep-flavored wine, such as a Sauvignon Blanc, to complement the rich saffron beurre blanc.

* Recipes not included.

Diane f Morgan

THREE-MUSHROOM SAUTÉ WITH CARAWAY CRISPS

Place the flour and salt in the workbowl of a food processor. Turn the machine on and off to combine. Cut the butter in 8 pieces and add to the workbowl. Pulse until the butter is the size of small peas. Add the cottage cheese and process just until the dough begins to form a ball. Shape into a disk, wrap in plastic wrap, and refrigerate for at least two hours or overnight.

Preheat oven to 375 degrees.

To roll out the dough, sprinkle the work surface with flour, then evenly distribute the caraway seeds, dill seeds, and dill weed. Roll out the dough to 1/8th inch thickness. Use a 1 1/2-inch scalloped biscuit cutter to cut out the crackers. Reroll the leftover dough with a bit more flour to make more crackers. Place them on lightly greased or non-stick cookie sheets about one inch apart. Brush the tops with a little extra virgin olive oil and sprinkle lightly with coarse salt. Bake for 20 minutes or until lightly browned on top. Let cool.

When ready to serve, warm the caraway crisps and heat 6 medium-sized plates.

To prepare the mushroom sauté, trim the stems of the mushrooms (remove the stems of the shiitake mushrooms altogether) and clean the mushrooms with a damp paper towel. Slice the mushrooms in half. If the chanterelles are large, cut in thirds or quarters so they are the same size as the other mushroom halves.

Melt the butter in a large sauté pan over high heat. Add the mushrooms and stir-cook until the mushrooms begin to give up some of their liquid. Sprinkle the salt, pepper, and sugar over the mushrooms and cook another 2 minutes. Add the balsamic vinegar. Then add the parsley and marjoram and stir-cook another minute.

To serve, divide the mushrooms among the 6 heated plates and arrange 4 to 6 of the caraway crisps around the mushrooms.

Makes 6 first course servings.

*Note: Although the spring and fall are the best times of year for obtaining fresh, exotic mushrooms, not all markets carry them. If you must substitute dried mushrooms for the chanterelles, use 2 ounces of dried porcini mushrooms. Soak the mushrooms, completely immersed, in warm water for 30 minutes, then rinse to remove any grit and pat dry. Proceed with the recipe as given above.

DM

DOUGH
1 cup all-purpose flour
1 teaspoon coarse salt
1/4 pound unsalted butter, well-chilled
1/2 cup creamed, small curd cottage cheese
....
Flour, for rolling out dough
2 tablespoons caraway seeds
1 tablespoon dill seeds
1 teaspoon dill weed
Extra virgin olive oil
Coarse salt
....

MUSHROOM SAUTÉ
1/2 pound chanterelle mushrooms*
1/2 pound shiitake mushrooms
1/2 pound white mushrooms
3 tablespoons unsalted butter
1/2 teaspoon coarse salt
Freshly ground black pepper, to taste
1 teaspoon sugar
2 tablespoons balsamic vinegar
4 tablespoons freshly minced Italian flat-leaf parsley
1 tablespoon freshly minced marjoram

1/2 cup good quality, dry white wine

1/3 cup rice wine vinegar

White part of 2 scallions, minced

1/4 teaspoon ground saffron, or threads of saffron crushed to make 1/4 teaspoon

2 sticks unsalted butter, cut in tablespoon-size bits

Coarse salt and freshly ground white pepper, to taste

1 medium to large tomato, peeled, seeded and diced 1/4-inch thick

················

1 shallot, minced

1 cup dry white wine

6 (4 to 5)-ounce sole fillets

FILLET OF SOLE WITH SAFFRON BEURRE BLANC

Sole is a remarkably "non-fishy" fish! It reminds me of scallops a little, although it is quite different in texture. Sand dabs and rex sole are two varieties that are very tasty and usually relatively inexpensive. The English, Dover, and petrale varieties are often more expensive. If you use sand or rex sole, you will have to contend with bones. As a result, this recipe is written for petrale, or any other fillet of sole, to make serving at the table easier!

To make the sauce, choose a medium, non-reactive saucepan. Place the liquids, scallions and saffron in the pan and boil down over medium-high heat until you have about 1/2 cup total volume left. Leaving the pan on the heat, add all the butter at one time. Remove from the heat as soon as the last solid bit of butter has melted into the sauce. The sauce should have emulsified to the point where it thinly coats a spoon. If you let the sauce boil, it will break down, leaving you with fancy melted butter. Stir in salt and pepper to taste. Add the diced tomatoes and set aside while you poach the fish.

*U*sing a wide, shallow pan, add the shallot, wine and enough water to fill the pan 1 1/2 inches deep. Bring to a simmer. Slide the fish into the simmering liquid and cook until the fish is just cooked in the middle, about 3 to 4 minutes for fillets that are approximately 1/2-inch thick at their thickest point. Lift the fish out of the water using a large slotted spoon or long, wide turner. Drain briefly on paper towels to remove excess water. Arrange the fish on individual serving plates and top with some sauce.

Serves 6.

Note: If you prefer, the fish can be lightly floured and sautéed instead of poached.

APPLE, ALMOND AND RAISIN TART

In the workbowl of a food processor fitted with the metal blade, place the flour, ground almonds, and salt. Pulse to combine. Add the butter and lard, and process until the butter is the size of small peas. Add 2 tablespoons of the beaten egg and the cider vinegar. With the machine running, add 2 to 3 tablespoons of the ice water. Process just until the dough begins to form a ball.

Lightly flour a work surface and rolling pin. Roll out the dough into a circle slightly larger than the tart pan. Fit the dough into the pan, crimp the edges, then refrigerate at least 30 minutes.

To make the filling, combine the first seven ingredients in a large sauté pan. Cover and cook over moderate heat until the apples are soft. Stir frequently. In the meantime, soak the raisins in Calvados to plump, and lightly toast the almonds. Reserve.

When the apples are tender, cool briefly. Remove the cinnamon stick and discard. Remove the vanilla bean, slit open, and scrape the inside of the bean into the apple mixture. Grind the apple mixture through a food mill. Add the Calvados and raisins, then mix in the toasted almonds. Reserve.

Preheat the oven to 425 degrees.

Line the pastry dough with foil and fill with pie weights, beans, or rice. Bake for 12 minutes. Remove the foil and pie weights, and bake until lightly browned. Cool.

Fill the pie shell with the apple mixture, smoothing the top. Slice the remaining apples and arrange in overlapping concentric circles, beginning along the outside edge. Brush the slices gently with the apple jelly. Sprinkle sugar generously over the top. Bake for 10 minutes. If the apples look dry, brush with more jelly. (I sometimes use a spray bottle filled with water to mist the apple slices.) Continue to bake until the apples are tender and the pie crust is nicely browned, about 20 to 25 more minutes.

Serve at room temperature accompanied by either a caramel or rich vanilla ice cream.

Serves 8 to 10.

PASTRY DOUGH
1 1/2 cups all-purpose flour
1/2 cup finely ground almonds
1 teaspoon coarse salt
1/4 pound unsalted butter, chilled, cut into eighths
3 tablespoons lard
1 small egg, beaten
1 teaspoon cider vinegar
2-3 tablespoons ice water
....

FILLING
6 yellow delicious apples, sliced
1/2 cup white dessert wine
1/2 cup sugar
1/4 teaspoon coarse salt
2 tablespoons unsalted butter
1-inch piece cinnamon stick
2-inch piece vanilla bean
2 tablespoons Calvados brandy
1/4 cup dark raisins
1/3 cup slivered almonds, toasted
....

3 additional apples
3 tablespoons apple jelly, melted
Sugar
....

Caramel or vanilla ice cream
....

11-inch tart pan with a removable bottom or
6 individual tart pans

AN INTERNATIONAL THANKSGIVING

Mussels in Cumin Vinaigrette
•
Herbed Chickpea Dip Served in an Artichoke
•
Pumpkin Tortellini
•
Cottage-Dill Focaccia
•
Roast Turkey with Greek Stuffing
•
Baked Fennel
•
Cranberry Ginger Chutney
•
Souffled Potatoes
•
Three Layer Ice Cream Bombe

*T*hanksgiving is a feast for all the senses. There are the wonderful aromas of turkey roasting and spicy pies baking in the oven. The eyes are dazzled by the beautiful array of food, flowers, silver, china, and crystal on the table. The eyes also enjoy the sight of relatives and friends. Our ears are pleased to hear their voices and laughter around the table. Hugs, kisses, handshakes – touching those we love is also an important part of the holiday.

But taste – ah, taste…!! After we have seen, heard, touched, and smelled Thanksgiving, we finally get to taste it! Certain flavors and ingredients are traditional on this day, and in our recipes we make use of them but in some new and different ways. However, Dan chose an untraditional beginning to this feast. He offers us two delicious hors d'oeuvres. One is an herbed chickpea dip served in an artichoke. The other is Mussels in a Cumin Vinaigrette. Both are as beautiful to the eye as they are pleasing to the tastebuds.

Bringing an international influence to this Thanksgiving, Kathleen uses pumpkin but as a filling for tortellini. Her Pumpkin Tortellini are scrumptious and a great first course. Of course we have roast turkey, but the rice stuffing has a Greek flavor with its combination of currants, chestnuts, lamb, and spices. Dan adds Souffled Potatoes and Diane supplies Baked Fennel in tomato sauce, Cranberry Ginger Chutney, and Cottage Dill Focaccia.

For dessert Kathleen dropped the "Bombe" – a wonderful Italian style concoction with three (count them) layers of homemade ice cream. Chocolate mocha, cinnamon, and *prune bourbon ice cream are layered in a rounded bowl shape.*

To help celebrate this occasion I would serve a lovely French Chablis with the hors d'oeurves and the first course. My suggestion for a wine to accompany the entrée would be a fine French Bordeaux or a California Cabernet Sauvignon. If you would prefer to offer a white wine with the turkey, a white Zinfandel would be nice.

This menu is truly a feast for all to enjoy in all the ways food can be enjoyed! Happy Thanksgiving to you all!!!

Georgia M. Vareldzis

MUSSELS IN CUMIN VINAIGRETTE

Mussels, those black-shelled beauties found on both coasts, are succulent little meats which lend themselves to all sorts of preparations. They are less chewy than clams and—on the West Coast, at least—often an attractive, bright orange color. They usually are sold with the "beards" (hair-like protein strands with which they attach themselves to rocks) removed. If not, grasp the "beard" as best you can and pull it away from the mussel. Then you're ready to proceed with the recipe. Serve it cold or at room temperature.

Place the cleaned mussels in a large saucepan with an inch of water. Bring the water to a boil, cover, and steam the mussels until their shells begin to open, approximately 5 minutes. Remove them from the heat and allow to cool while you make the dressing. Discard any unopened mussels.

To make the dressing, first toast the ground cumin in a heavy-bottomed small skillet until it is aromatic but not burned, approximately 3 to 5 minutes. Then place all the dressing ingredients in a pint jar with a tight-fitting lid and shake vigorously. Taste and adjust the seasonings to your liking.

Remove the mussels from their shells, saving half of each shell for presentation. Toss the mussels with the dressing and allow to stand for 30 minutes before serving. The mussels can be stored for up to 2 days in the refrigerator.

To serve, place mussel shells on a serving platter. Put one mussel meat into each shell and top with a little extra dressing. Sprinkle with a little extra minced parsley.

Serves 6 to 8.

2 dozen uniformly-sized mussels, shells washed and debearded

. . . .

1 teaspoon ground cumin, dry skillet toasted
3 tablespoons sherry vinegar
2 teaspoons dijon-style mustard
1/2 teaspoon sugar
1/2 teaspoon coarse salt
1 clove fresh garlic, finely minced
1 tablespoon finely minced onion
2 tablespoons minced parsley
1/2 cup plus 1 tablespoon extra virgin olive oil

. . . .

Extra minced parsley for garnish

HERBED CHICKPEA DIP

1 large artichoke, trimmed, drizzled with lemon juice and steamed over simmering water just until tender. Hollow-out the center when cool.

·················

3/4 cup good quality olive oil
3 tablespoons fresh rosemary leaves or
1 tablespoon dry
1 can garbanzo beans (chickpeas), drained and rinsed
3 large cloves garlic, peeled
3/4 cup minced parsley
1 tablespoon minced fresh mint or
1 teaspoon dry

·················

Toasted Pita Chips, or
Freshly cut raw vegetables, or
Bread sticks

Middle Eastern "hummus" is the inspiration for this recipe. I dearly love the silky-textured hummus I've eaten in several Lebanese restaurants. Embellishing on the original here, I believe you'll find one bite leads to another!

For this Thanksgiving feast I have chosen to serve this chickpea dip in a trimmed, hollowed-out, cooked artichoke. It makes a lovely presentation, and the leaves can be dipped in the spread. However, if you are short on time, place the chickpea dip in an attractive bowl and garnish with a sprig of fresh mint.

In a small pan, heat the olive oil and the rosemary until it is quite warm but not smoking. Continue to "cook" the herb in the oil for 5 to 10 minutes and remove from the heat. Strain the oil and discard the rosemary.

*I*n a food processor or blender, purée the garbanzo beans and garlic to a very smooth texture, adding the herbed olive oil during the process. Add the parsley and mint. Taste and adjust the seasonings. Serve with a selection of toasted pita chips, freshly cut vegetables (including extra artichoke leaves), or bread sticks.

Serves 6 to 8.

PUMPKIN TORTELLINI

Tradition meets innovation in this first course recipe. Pumpkin has always found its way into Thanksgiving, but here we use it in an Italian-style stuffed pasta. The fresh pasta for the tortellini can be made at home or purchased in sheets if these are available. If you make the pasta, it can be prepared in advance and frozen. Be sure to cook it directly from the freezer.

To make the filling, place the Amaretti cookies and dried fruit in the workbowl of a food processor fitted with a metal blade. Process until finely chopped. Add the remaining ingredients and process until well blended. This filling can be made a couple of days before making the tortellini. It can also be frozen several weeks before using.

If making your own pasta, place the flour in the workbowl of a processor fitted with the metal blade. Drop the eggs on top of the flour and then begin to process. Add only enough water so that the pasta dough is not crumbly when pressed together between two fingers. Stop the machine while processing and check consistency.

Remove the dough from the processor and form into a ball. Break off large walnut-sized pieces of dough and run them through a hand crank or electric pasta machine until thin sheets are formed. Make the sheets as wide as possible. (Roll out only one sheet at a time, keeping the rest of the dough ball covered with plastic wrap.) With a rolling pastry cutter or knife, cut the sheet of dough into approximately 2 1/2-inch squares. Taking one square at a time, wet your index finger with water and moisten two adjoining sides of the square. Place a 1/2 teaspoon of filling in the center of the square. Bring the dry and the wet corner together. Fold the two bottom ends of the triangle over your finger and press together. Bend the top corner over so that the tortellini looks like a jaunty little hat. As you complete each one, place them on a greased cookie sheet.

When ready to cook, bring 12 quarts of water to a boil in a large stockpot. Add a couple of tablespoons of salt. Gently put the tortellini into the boiling water and boil until they rise to the surface. At this point they should be done, but it is still wise to test one to be sure.

Pour them very gently (they are fragile!) into a large colander and drain thoroughly. Transfer them to a large, wide bowl. Drizzle with the extra virgin olive oil and a couple of tablespoons of grated cheese. Toss very gently and then portion into individual heated serving bowls. Sprinkle each serving with a little more grated cheese and serve at once.

Makes 10 to 11 dozen tortellini (should serve 12 to 16 people).

K. T.

FILLING
2 Amaretti cookies
(or other dry almond cookie)
2 ounces dried pineapple or apricots
2 cups canned pumpkin (not pie filling)
2 teaspoons Dijon mustard
3 ounces grated aged Provolone or imported Parmesan
1 teaspoon coarse salt
2 tablespoons bread crumbs

· · · · · · · · · · · · · · · · ·

PASTA
3 cups all-purpose flour
3 large eggs
Water

· · · · · · · · · · · · · · · · ·

Extra virgin olive oil
Grated, dry aged cheese, Provolone or imported Parmesan

1 package yeast
1/4 cup warm water
Pinch sugar
1 cup small curd cottage cheese, slightly warmed
2 tablespoons sugar
1 tablespoons instant dried onions
1 tablespoon melted butter
1 tablespoon dill seeds
1 tablespoon dill weed
1 tablespoon dried Italian herbs
1 teaspoon coarse salt
1/4 teaspoon baking soda
1 unbeaten egg
2 cups all-purpose flour
1/2 cup yellow cornmeal
....

3 tablespoons fruity olive oil

COTTAGE DILL FOCACCIA

Bread is not usually served during a Thanksgiving feast because turkey often has a bread stuffing of sorts. However, since Georgia developed a Greek rice stuffing for the turkey, we thought it would be nice to serve a bread with the first course. This bread is SIMPLE to make. It is referred to as a batter bread because there is no kneading involved. It is just a matter of mixing the dough, letting it rise, and baking it. And it is wonderful with the Pumpkin Tortellini.

Dissolve the yeast in the warm water, then sprinkle in a pinch of sugar. Let this mixture "proof" for a few minutes to be sure the yeast is active. Warm the cottage cheese in a microwave, making sure it is not hot. Mix together the cottage cheese and yeast mixture, using a mixer with a dough hook or a large mixing bowl and wooden spoon. Beat in the rest of the ingredients. The dough will be quite sticky. Cover and let rise in a warm place until it has doubled in bulk, about one hour.

*F*or baking the bread, a cast-iron pan works the best, but a heavy-gauge metal one will do. Grease a large 12-inch skillet thoroughly with the olive oil, leaving any excess in the pan. Stir down the dough and place in the pan. Using your finger tips, press the dough to flatten it and spread it out to the edges of the pan. Let it rise again until not quite doubled in bulk, about 40 minutes.

*B*ake in a preheated 350-degree oven until nicely browned, about 40 minutes. Remove to a cooling rack, brush with additional olive oil, and sprinkle with some additional coarse salt.

*C*ut in wedges when ready to serve. The bread can be rewarmed, if you like, but it is quite tasty at room temperature.

Serves 8 to 10.

DM

ROAST TURKEY WITH GREEK STUFFING

I make the broth for the stuffing by boiling the turkey neck, wing tips, and gizzard. Cover these parts with water in a large pot and simmer until the neck and gizzard are tender. Strain and skim off any fat. Set aside. Any broth you don't use for the stuffing can be frozen and used to cook rice or in soup.

In a sauté pan or large frying pan, melt the butter. When it is foamy, add the onion, green onions, celery, and parsley and cook over medium-low heat until they become transparent and tender, about 10 minutes.

Add the ground meat and liver, and cook over medium heat until the ground meat is browned.

Add the chestnuts (or toasted pinenuts, if using them), currants, rice and the broth. Bring to a boil and simmer, uncovered, until nearly all the liquid is absorbed, about 10 to 15 minutes. (The rice will still be firm at this stage). Add the allspice, salt, and pepper, and set aside to cool completely before stuffing the turkey. The stuffing can be made up to 2 days ahead and refrigerated. Bring to room temperature before stuffing the turkey.

Bring the turkey to room temperature. After washing, rub the cavity with salt and pepper. Squeeze the juice from the lemon and pour into the cavity. Rub the outside of the turkey with olive oil.

Immediately prior to roasting, stuff the turkey carefully, allowing room for the rice to expand. Sew or clamp the opening shut. If using a turkey breast, place the stuffing under the breast to roast. Any extra stuffing can be baked in a casserole dish.

Roast the turkey at 325 degrees until a meat thermometer placed into the thigh meat reads 170 to 175 degrees. Time will vary according to the weight of the turkey. (When we tested a 14-pound turkey, it tested done in 3 1/2 hours.) If roasting a whole breast, roast in a covered pan and uncover the last 30 minutes to brown the skin.

The excess stuffing can be basted with drippings from the turkey. Allow the cooked turkey to stand for 20 minutes before carving.

This recipe serves 8 to 14 depending on the size of the turkey.

* You may substitute 1/2 cup toasted pine nuts if you prefer.

YEMESI (GREEK STUFFING)
4 tablespoons butter
1 large onion, chopped
1 bunch green onions, chopped
3 stalks celery (including leaves), chopped
1/4 cup minced parsley
1 pound ground lamb or beef
Liver from the turkey or 1/4 pound of chicken livers, chopped
8 ounces fresh chestnuts*, boiled or roasted, then peeled and chopped
1 cup dried currants
1 cup long grain white rice
2 cups chicken broth
1/2 teaspoon ground allspice
1 teaspoon coarse salt
Freshly ground black pepper, to taste

· · · · · · · · · · · · · · · · · ·

1 (12 to 18 pound) turkey, or whole uncooked turkey breast
Salt and pepper
Juice of one lemon
1/4 cup olive oil

6 large fennel bulbs

1/3 cup fruity olive oil

1 large onion, peeled, root end sliced off, then cut into thin wedges

3 medium garlic cloves, minced

3 large tomatoes, blanched to remove skin, seeded and diced

2 tablespoons finely minced fresh parsley

1 teaspoon coarse salt

1/2 teaspoon sugar

Freshly ground black pepper, to taste

· · · · · · · · · · · · · · · · ·

CRUMB TOPPING

1/2 cup dry bread crumbs

1/2 cup freshly grated Parmesan cheese

1 teaspoon thyme

1/2 teaspoon coarse salt

BAKED FENNEL

Creating different recipes from the limited supply of winter produce can be a challenge. I have always felt that fennel is one of the more overlooked of the season's vegetables. This vegetable dish has been a part of my Thanksgiving table for quite a few years. So I thought I would share this recipe with you and hope that you will discover just how good fennel can be.

Remove the stalks from the fennel bulb and discard. Use a vegetable peeler to remove any browned areas on the outside layers of the bulb. Cut the fennel in half vertically. Cut out the core and discard. Clean the layers of the fennel, then slice into thin wedges as was done for the onion.

*I*n a large sauté pan, heat the olive oil over medium-high heat. Add the fennel, onion, and garlic and sauté until it is crisp-tender, about 5 to 7 minutes. Stir frequently. Turn down the heat if it begins to brown. Add the tomato, parsley, and seasonings and stir-cook an additional 3 to 4 minutes. Taste and adjust seasonings.

*P*repare the crumb topping by mixing together the bread crumbs, Parmesan, thyme, and salt. Reserve.

*P*lace the fennel mixture in a decorative, shallow, oven-to-table dish. Spread the crumb topping evenly over the top. This dish can be prepared up to this point and set aside at room temperature for several hours before baking.

*P*reheat the oven to 375 degrees. Bake the dish in the top third of the oven for 30 minutes or until nicely browned. Check it at the halfway point to make sure it is not browning too much. If it is, place on a lower oven rack.

Serves 6 to 8.

DM

CRANBERRY GINGER CHUTNEY

This is a variation on the Cranberry Chutney that appeared in our first book. Ever since I made my first cranberry chutney, I have been hard-pressed to go back to the more traditional cranberry sauce or relish which most often appears on the holiday table. This time, I've given the chutney a quasi-Chinese flavor with the addition of preserved ginger. This chutney will keep for at least six months under refrigeration...if it lasts that long!

In a large, deep saucepan combine the first 6 ingredients. Bring to a boil, stirring frequently, and cook 10 to 15 minutes or until the berries pop. Add the apples, pears, onion, raisins, and ginger and continue cooking, stirring frequently, until thick. This may take up to 15 minutes. Remove from the heat and add the cashews and orange zest. Let cool completely. Discard the cinnamon sticks and cloves, if you can find them. Refrigerate in covered jars until ready to use.

Makes about 2 quarts.

* This can be found in Chinese markets as whole preserved ginger in syrup. It usually comes in these wonderful little green-glazed ceramic jars that are tied with twine. The preserved ginger seems to keep indefinitely.

DM

4 cups whole cranberries (fresh or frozen)
2 1/2 cups sugar
1 1/4 cups water
6 whole cloves
2 cinnamon sticks
1 teaspoon coarse salt
2 tart apples (preferably Newton or Granny Smith), peeled, cored and diced
2 firm pears, peeled, cored and diced
1 small onion, diced
1 cup golden raisins
1/3 cup chopped, preserved ginger in syrup*
1/2 cup very large cashews, toasted
1 1/2 tablespoons grated orange rind

2 1/2 to 3 pounds russet ("baking") potatoes
8 ounces (2 sticks) unsalted butter, at room temperature
4 large eggs
1/2 cup minced onion
12 to 18 fresh sage leaves, chopped, or
2 teaspoons dried, crushed
1 teaspoon coarse salt
8 to 10 grinds fresh pepper

SOUFFLED POTATOES

Here is an easy dish to make that can be done a day or two ahead except for the final cooking. In a way it amounts to mashed potatoes, but the presentation gets a lot more attention at the table!

Preheat an oven to 450 degrees. Have the oven rack in the middle of the oven.

Pierce each potato several times with a fork or skewer. Place the potatoes on the middle oven rack and bake until they are thoroughly cooked, about 45 to 50 minutes if they are medium sized. Remove the potatoes from the oven and allow to cool just until they can be handled. (Don't allow the potatoes to cool completely in their jackets; they are easier to work with when they are still hot and mealy.)

Scrape the pulp from the skins. Using a large, open wire whisk or a mixer fitted with the pastry paddle, combine all ingredients well.

Spread the mixture in a shallow, buttered 10 to 12-inch oven to table dish. I use a 10-inch porcelain quiche dish. The potatoes fill it completely as they puff during baking, threatening to overflow the sides.

Reduce the oven heat to 400 degrees. Place the baking dish on a baking sheet to catch any drips. Bake about 30 minutes until nicely browned on top; use the broiler for the final browning if necessary. Serve at once.

Note: If you are serving this with the turkey, it may be baked while the turkey rests (covered) before being carved. Just adjust the oven up to 400 degrees immediately upon removing the bird!

Serves 8 to 10.

THREE LAYER ICE CREAM BOMBE

This three-layer ice cream bombe is a wonderful way to end a VERY filling Thanksgiving meal. It is relatively light, especially if cut in thin wedges. Any combination of your favorite ice creams can be used. Just remember to think of complementary colors and flavors when planning to make a bombe. You wouldn't want three pale-colored ice creams or three citrus flavors together. The individual components can be made ahead of time and frozen. Even the bombe can be assembled weeks in advance and frozen. If time is tight, store-bought ice cream can be used.

To make the Mocha Glace, bring the espresso and sugar to a boil in a 1-quart saucepan. Allow it to boil vigorously for 4 minutes . Add the bittersweet chocolate and remove from the heat, stirring until the chocolate is melted.

Whip the cream until it holds soft peaks. Set aside so that it can warm slightly. In the meantime, beat the yolks until light colored, about 2 minutes. While still beating, pour the hot chocolate mixture into the beaten yolks, and beat until very smooth. Allow to cool to room temperature.

If the whipped cream has separated at all, whisk gently with a wire whisk to recombine. With a rubber spatula gently fold the whipped cream into the chocolate mixture. Refrigerate for a couple of hours. Freeze in an ice cream maker according to the manufacturer's directions.

To make the Bourbon Prune Ice Cream, drain the bourbon-soaked prunes, and then purée the prunes in a food processor. You should have 1 1/2 cups of purée. Stir in the chopped toasted hazelnuts. Whip the heavy cream with the sugar until soft peaks form and then fold this mixture into the prune purée. Freeze in an ice cream machine according to the manufacturer's directions. This ice cream will never freeze very hard because of the high proportion of alcohol in it.

The bombe can be assembled in a plain 2-quart metal bowl or in one of the lovely molds designed specifically as ice cream molds. If you are using a plain metal bowl, smoothly line the bowl with plastic wrap, to allow for easier unmolding. Start assembling the bombe with the Mocha Glace. With each layer allow the ice cream you are working with to soften in the refrigerator for about 20 minutes. Using a large, wide-bottomed spoon, spread a layer of Mocha Glace about 3/4-inch thick around the bottom and up the sides of the bowl. Try to spread it as evenly as possible. Cover with plastic wrap and place back in a very cold freezer for 1 to 2 hours (or longer). Follow the same procedure with the Cinnamon ice cream, again allowing the bombe to freeze firmly after working with it. Finally, place the Bourbon Prune ice cream in the center. If the bombe is being assembled a week or so before serving, wrap tightly and place in the coldest part of the freezer.

On the day of serving, dip the bowl or mold briefly into hot water once or twice until it will unmold. Place it onto a nice serving platter. Smooth the top and return the bombe to the freezer to harden again. Just before serving, pipe some whipped cream rosettes around the base and on the top of the mold. Serve on chilled plates.

Serves 12.

Note: You will have more Mocha Glace and Cinnamon ice cream than you need to form the bombe, but who's arguing?

K. T.

Ice Cream #1
MOCHA GLACE
3/4 cup strong espresso
1/3 cup granulated sugar
8 ounces bittersweet chocolate, finely chopped (Guittard is excellent)
2 cups heavy cream
4 large egg yolks
. . . .

Ice Cream #2
CINNAMON MAPLE from Indulgence menu
. . . .

Ice Cream #3
BOURBON PRUNE WITH TOASTED HAZELNUTS
2 cups pitted prunes that have been soaked in 2/3 cup of bourbon for at least one week
1/4 cup chopped toasted hazelnuts (skinned as best you can)
2/3 cup heavy cream
2 tablespoons granulated sugar
. . . .

Whipped cream, for garnish

AN INTERNATIONAL THANKSGIVING

COME FOR BRUNCH

I am writing this introduction while enjoying a café latté and a pineapple-oat bran muffin, and I am thinking of all the reasons why I enjoy cooking brunch. Breakfast is out as a time for entertaining– after all, who wants to get up even earlier to prepare food for guests? Lunch is a possibility, of course, but I think I'll croak if I see one more variation on chicken salad or pita-stuffed sandwiches. While it may sound like I've arrived at the idea of brunch through a process of elimination, the real reason why I like cooking brunch is because the possibilities for an interesting menu are so much greater.

Skewered Fruit with a Saffron-Cognac Sauce
•
Stuffed Brunch Braid
•
Smoked Salmon Blintzes with Sour Cream and Chives
•
Chocolate Nut Berry Bread

When this cooking foursome got together to work on a brunch menu, the recipe ideas flew. Kathleen loves fruit, so it was her choice to offer an atypical, but delicious, recipe for Skewered Fruit with a Saffron-Cognac Sauce. The sauce can easily be made a day or two ahead and refrigerated. The fruit looks attractive on skewers, but it can also be thinly sliced and served on fruit plates.

Georgia had an idea for a Stuffed Brunch Braid. After a few tries (yes, even professional cooks don't always produce a winner the first time, it's just that some are more willing to admit it than others!), she developed a very attractive loaf that is stuffed with goat cheese, black forest ham, and roasted sweet red pepper. Our recommendation is to either make it ahead and freeze it or, preferably, to make the dough and filling the night before and refrigerate it. Then the morning of the brunch, let the bread rise, stuff it, and bake it fresh for your guests.

I was having lunch at a trendy Pittsburgh restaurant– is that an oxymoron?– and ordered Smoked Salmon Blintzes for my appetizer. I liked the taste combination of lox, dairy, and chives and made some notes. Upon returning home, I developed the recipe. The nice part about this recipe is that the blintzes really freeze well and just need to be sautéed the day of the brunch.

Now, Dan, our famous bread baker, was assigned the task of creating a quick bread. He claims his forte is yeast breads, but he did just fine with a little baking powder. His Chocolate Nut Berry Bread was so good, we rewarded him with requests for seconds...your guests will too. This bread also freezes well.

Sounds like an easy menu to me—think I'll sleep in an extra hour!

Diane J. Morgan

SKEWERED FRUIT WITH A SAFFRON-COGNAC SAUCE

Fresh fruits are a must for me in the morning, and this recipe dresses them up a little. Use seasonal fruits. For a winter brunch, use bananas, pineapple, and kiwis. For a summer brunch, your choices of fruit are unlimited. Just remember to vary the colors for the prettiest effect. If time allows, you can arrange the fruit on small bamboo skewers, serving about three skewers per person. Serve the Saffron-Cognac Sauce in a little ramekin on the side. But if you are short on time, the fruits are equally delicious served in small bowls with the sauce drizzled on top.

Beat the egg yolks with the sugar until thick and pale yellow. Place the milk and cream in a heavy 2-quart saucepan with the saffron and salt.

Whisk in the cornstarch. Place over medium-low heat and bring the milk/cream mixture to 150 degrees on an instant read thermometer, stirring regularly.

Beating vigorously, add about half of the hot milk/cream mixture to the egg yolks. Pour this mixture back into the saucepan and return to the heat. Bring the temperature of the custard to 170 degrees while stirring constantly. Turn off the heat. Continue to stir for a minute or so. Let the mixture cool. Add the vanilla and cognac and chill well.

Serve with fresh skewered fruit.

Makes sauce for 6 servings of fruit.

K. T.

5 large egg yolks
1/3 cup sugar
1 cup milk
1 cup heavy cream
1/4 teaspoon powdered saffron
Pinch salt
1 tablespoon cornstarch
1/2 teaspoon pure vanilla extract
1 teaspoon cognac

DOUGH

1 package dry yeast

1/2 cup plus 2 tablespoons warm water (105 to 115 degrees)

1 teaspoon sugar

2 cups bread flour

1 cup whole wheat flour

1 teaspoon coarse salt

2 tablespoons unsalted butter, at room temperature

1 egg, beaten

. . . .

FILLING

8 ounces Black Forest ham

1 tablespoon chopped fresh mint, or 1 teaspoon dried

5 1/2 ounces Montrachet or other goat cheese

1 roasted sweet red pepper

1 tablespoon olive oil

. . . .

GLAZE

1 egg, beaten

STUFFED BRUNCH BRAID

Dissolve the yeast in warm water with the sugar and set aside until it foams, (about 5 minutes). Heat oven to lowest setting and turn off.

*I*n the workbowl of a food processor, place the flours and salt. Cut the butter into 3 pieces and process with the flour for 30 seconds. Add the egg to the yeast mixture, and then pour this mixture through the feed-tube while the machine is running. Add the liquid mixture slowly so it is absorbed into the flour. When the dough cleans the sides of the workbowl, process it for 45 more seconds. (This is the kneading process.) Remove the dough from the workbowl and place it in a large (1-gallon size) plastic bag. Press to remove air and tie at the *top*, so the dough has room to expand. Place in a warm spot and allow to rise until doubled, about 45 minutes.

*M*eanwhile, finely dice the ham into 1/4-inch pieces. Mix the mint with the cheese and set aside. To roast a red pepper, singe over a flame or under the broiler until the skin has blackened. Place in a plastic bag and put into the freezer for about 10 minutes. Remove and scrape off the skin, remove ends and seeds. Dice the red pepper and set aside.

*W*hen the dough has risen, remove from the bag. Roll out on a floured board into a 10x16 rectangle. Place on a greased baking pan or cookie sheet. Brush the center third lengthwise, with olive oil. Spread the cheese-mint mixture over the top of the olive oil. Distribute the ham and then the red pepper evenly over the cheese. With a sharp knife, make 1-inch horizontal cuts in the dough from the filling to the outer edge. Overlap these strips of dough over the center, alternating sides. Allow to rise until double.

*B*rush with the glaze. Bake in a preheated 400-degree oven until nicely browned, about 25 to 30 minutes. With a large spatula, carefully move the braid to a cooling rack. This bread can be served hot, warm, or at room temperature. It can also be frozen after it cools. Reheat it in a 300-degree oven for about 30 minutes.

Serves 10 to 12, depending on the size of the slices.

Stuffed Brunch Braid

BATTER

1 1/2 cups all-purpose flour, measured, then sifted
1 1/2 teaspoons coarse salt
2 teaspoons baking powder
Freshly ground white pepper, to taste
4 eggs
1 1/3 cups milk
1 cup water
3 tablespoons finely chopped chives

....

FILLING

16 ounces dry curd cottage cheese
16 ounces small curd cottage cheese
3 egg yolks
Zest of 1 lemon, about 1 1/2 teaspoons
Freshly ground white pepper, to taste
2 tablespoons finely chopped chives
1/2 pound sliced Nova Scotia lox, finely diced

....

3 tablespoons butter
5 tablespoons corn oil, divided

....

1 pint sour cream
Fresh chives, finely chopped, for garnish

SMOKED SALMON BLINTZES WITH SOUR CREAM AND CHIVES

Resift the flour with the salt, baking powder, and pepper into a large bowl. In a separate bowl beat the eggs, and then add the milk, water, and chives. Make a well in the sifted ingredients, pour in the liquid ingredients, and combine with a few swift strokes. Ignore the lumps, they will dissolve when you stir the batter before making the crepes. Let the batter rest for 30 minutes at room temperature.

While the batter is resting make the filling. In the workbowl of a food processor combine the two types of cottage cheese, the egg yolks, lemon zest, and pepper. Process for one minute. Remove to a medium-sized bowl and gently stir in the lox and chives. Taste and adjust seasonings if necessary.

Using a 5 to 6-inch crepe pan make the crepes. Allow about 3 tablespoons of batter per crepe. Have the pan well-heated before beginning. Using about 2 tablespoons of the oil, brush the pan with a little of the oil before adding batter each time. Cook each crepe on one side until lightly browned, then turn and cook just a few seconds on the other side. Remove to waxed paper to cool. As the pancakes cool, stake between sheets of waxed paper.

Divide the filling among the crepes, allowing about 1/4 cup per crepe. Fold up envelope-style, by first folding the bottom to cover the filling, then folding over the two sides. Allow the seam to be on the bottom of the blintz. (The blintzes can be made to this point ahead of time and refrigerated or frozen.)

In a 10-inch skillet heat one tablespoon each of the butter and oil. Sauté the blintzes over medium heat, allowing them to brown nicely on both sides. Add more butter and oil to the pan as needed. Keep warm in a 200-degree oven while completing the batches.

When ready to serve, stir the sour cream until smooth and creamy. Place two blintzes in the center of a warmed plate, spoon sour cream over them and garnish with the chives.

Makes about 24 blintzes.

DM

CHOCOLATE NUT BERRY BREAD

Preheat oven to 350 degrees. Butter and flour two 4x8-inch loaf pans. Mix together the flours, baking powder, baking soda, salt, cinnamon and mace and set aside.

Mix the butter, eggs, zest, orange juice, and brown sugar well. Stir in the nuts and chocolate chips. Then stir in flour mixture.

Gently fold in the blueberries. Divide the batter between the prepared pans and bake for 55-65 minutes or until a tester comes out clean or an instant-read thermometer reads at least 180 degrees. Remove from pan after five minutes and cool on a rack.

Makes 2 loaves.

2 cups all-purpose flour
1 1/2 cups cake flour
1 tablespoon baking powder
1/2 teaspoon baking soda
1 teaspoon coarse salt
1 teaspoon cinnamon
1/4 teaspoon ground mace
1 stick (4 ounces) unsalted butter, at room temperature
3 large eggs
Zest of 1 orange, grated or finely chopped
1/2 cup orange juice
1 1/3 cups brown sugar
1 cup coarsely chopped hazelnuts
1 cup semisweet chocolate chips
1 cup blueberries

OUR CHRISTMAS DINNER

Bacon-Wrapped
Prunes
•
Blue Cheese Pastry
Buttons
•
Fillet of Sole
Romanoff
•
Prime Rib of Beef
with Horseradish
•
Roasted Potatoes
•
Julienne of Beets
•
Greek Christmas
Bread
•
Chocolate Cranberry
Christmas Roulade

*I*f smell has a lot to do with memory, as I am convinced that it does, then it follows that the smells of CHRISTMAS set off a storehouse of memories in most people living in North America. My earliest memories of Christmastime are forever linked to the smell of pine from the Christmas tree, wreaths, and table decorations used in our home, a parsonage attached to a small church that my father served. I recall the Swedes in our congregation whenever I smell the combination of coffee and Christmas cookies and cakes. The smells of baking ham studded with cloves and roasting turkey make me think of my mother. She busied herself with cooking and baking for the holiday pot-luck suppers at the church. I can still recall the smell of the scalloped potato dishes she often made at this time of year.

Kathleen, Diane, and Georgia all recall the smell of sweets such as butter cookies and gingerbread when they think of Christmas. Like millions of others, they were seduced by the aromas of butter, flour, and sugar baking in a hot oven. It is no surprise then that some of them have written recipes for sweet foods for the holiday.

Our menu begins with two wonderful appetizers. Diane's Blue Cheese Pastry Buttons are a snap to prepare. A few minutes spent with a rolling pin and a floured countertop will produce a memorably crispy beginning to your special meal. Kathleen's Bacon-Wrapped Prunes are seductive, being slightly sweet and smoky at the same time. Georgia's Greek Christmas Bread is also slightly sweet and perfumed with cardamom or mahlep. We thought a simple but elegant first course of Fillet of Sole Romanoff would set the right tone for this special occasion. Prime Rib of Beef is our entrée, accompanied by baby Roasted Potatoes, and a bright red Julienne of Beets tossed in butter. The smell of the

Roasted Potatoes, and a bright red Julienne of Beets tossed in butter. The smell of the roasting beef will conjure up memories of special times past for lots of us! Diane's Chocolate Cranberry Christmas Roulade tops off what we hope will be a meal so special that its memory will bring a smile to your face years from now! Merry Christmas to all, especially to the cook!

BACON-WRAPPED PRUNES

I beg you to try these! I have to because it's probably the only way you will. But I promise you they're wonderful. Years ago when Dan and I were catering, I often used to try to convince a hostess to let us serve a version of these as an appetizer. Rarely was I successful. But when I was, everyone loved them. They are a great combination of sweet, salty, and creamy—a masterful little mouthful!

Partially cook the bacon slices. If you have a microwave, put the oven on full power for about 1 1/2 minutes. This will render some of the fat and allow the bacon to begin to shrivel. Cool the bacon.

In the meantime blend the cream cheese, ricotta cheese, Tabasco, and sage in a food processor until smooth and well blended. I generally use a small knife to stuff the cheese mixture in the prunes, but you might be more comfortable with a small spoon. Round the cheese on top of the prune opening (it will firm as it cooks).

Cut the bacon slices in half lengthwise. Then wrap a slice of bacon around each stuffed prune. (These may be prepared a couple of days in advance up to this point and refrigerated.)

Preheat the oven to 450 degrees. Place prunes (as many as you want to cook at a time) on a cookie sheet. Bake for approximately 7 minutes or until the bacon is nice and crisp. Allow to cool for at *least* five minutes before serving. Otherwise you might be responsible for some badly burned tongues.

Makes 4 dozen.

K. T.

24 slices good-quality bacon
4 ounces cream cheese
1/2 cup whole milk ricotta cheese
1/2 teaspoon Tabasco
24 large fresh sage leaves
48 large pitted prunes

2/3 cup unbleached white flour
1/2 teaspoon coarse salt
1/8 teaspoon freshly ground black pepper
3 tablespoons unsalted butter, cold
2/3 cup grated, sharp cheddar cheese
3 tablespoons sour cream
....
1/2 cup blue cheese, room temperature
2 tablespoons unsalted butter, room temperature

BLUE CHEESE PASTRY BUTTONS

When I am working on a new recipe or developing a menu, I often reflect on memorable meals I have had in restaurants. For this recipe, I thought about the tiny appetizers that we were served at Le Perroquet in Chicago. These little crackers garnished with a rosette of blue cheese butter make a wonderful beginning to a Christmas dinner.

Put the flour, salt, and pepper in the workbowl of a food processor and pulse to combine. Add the butter, cheddar cheese, and sour cream and process until the dough begins to form a ball. Remove from the workbowl, flatten between two pieces of plastic wrap, and refrigerate for 30 minutes.

Preheat the oven to 350 degrees.

In the meantime, wipe the workbowl clean and process the blue cheese and butter until completely combined. Remove to a small bowl and reserve.

On a lightly floured surface, roll out the dough until it is 1/8-inch thick. Use a 1 1/2-inch fluted cookie cutter to cut the crackers. Reroll the dough to cut more crackers. Place the crackers on nonstick or lightly greased cookie sheets. Use a fork to prick the dough all over before baking. Bake for 10 to 12 minutes or until lightly browned on the bottom. Remove to a cooling rack. (These crackers will keep for several days in a tightly sealed tin, but I suggest rebaking them for 3 minutes on the day you wish to serve them.)

To serve, place the blue cheese butter (which should be at room temperature) in a pastry bag fitted with a no. 18 tip. Make a tiny rosette of butter in the center of each cracker. Pass on a serving tray.

Makes about 60.

DM

NEW YEAR'S RESOLUTION

HAPPY NEW YEAR!! Now, where's my list of resolutions from last year? I might as well look at them again because they are the same old resolutions that I made last year, and the year before that, and... Oh well, let's see if I can stick to them this year! First on my list and, I suspect, on most people's lists is to GO ON A DIET!! All is not lost—here we offer two menus that are not only light but beautiful to look at and so tasty you'll wonder if we know what we're talking about!

Curried Cauliflower Soup
•
Greek Fish Plaki
•
Grapefruit Sorbet

Diane starts off the first menu with a wonderful Curried Cauliflower Soup. Greek Fish Plaki is the main course. The fillets are baked in an olive oil-seasoned tomato sauce with carrots and potatoes—a one-dish meal. Grapefruit Sorbet completes the meal and is a great complement to the fish.

Fresh Green Bean and Shallot Salad
•
Oriental Seared Beef with Vegetables
•
Chocolate Lingonberry Dacquoise

Diane again begins the second menu with Fresh Green Bean and Shallot Salad seasoned without oil. Dan's Oriental Seared Beef with Vegetables is unbelievably beautiful. The slices of rare beef, vegetables and accompanying sauce make for a delicious, satisfying meal. Cocoa-flavored meringues topped with lingonberry preserves and slightly sweetened ricotta cheese comprise Kathleen's dessert dacquoise.

Set the table with flowers and your prettiest dishes and placemats. Enjoy the beauty of the food and its wonderful flavors. Sticking to my diet is going to be easier than I thought!!!

Georgia M. Vareldzis

CURRIED CAULIFLOWER SOUP

1 tablespoon olive oil
1 medium onion, diced
1 1/2 tablespoons curry powder
1 tablespoon sugar
1 1/2 teaspoons coarse salt
Freshly ground white pepper, to taste
2 medium new potatoes, peeled and chunked
1 medium head cauliflower, flowerets only, chunked
6 cups defatted chicken stock
2 cups low-fat plain yogurt, room temperature
2 tablespoons freshly minced parsley

It will surprise your guests that this is a low-calorie, low-fat soup!

In a 6-quart soup pot, heat the olive oil. Add the onion and sauté covered for about 5 minutes. Stir frequently. Add the curry, sugar, salt, and pepper and sauté another minute.

Add the potatoes, cauliflower, and stock. Bring to a simmer and cook, covered, until the vegetables are tender, about 30 to 40 minutes. Let cool briefly, then put through a food mill or purée in a blender or food processor. Return to the soup pot and when ready to serve, stir in the yogurt and parsley. Serve hot, but do not let the soup boil.

Serves 6 to 8.

DM

FISH PLAKI

In a large frying pan, preferably nonstick, heat the olive oil. Turn heat to medium and add the garlic, onion, green onions, celery, and carrots. Also add the potatoes if you are using them. Sauté until the vegetables are glazed and soft, about 5 minutes, then cover and allow to cook over medium heat for about 10 minutes. This process "steam fries" the vegetables, eliminating the need for more oil. It is often called "sweating".

Add the spinach, tomato sauce, salt, pepper, and minced parsley. Cover and simmer for 15 minutes.

Spoon half the vegetable mixture into a baking dish. Top with the fish and cover with the remaining mixture. Keep fish in a single layer.

Cover and bake in a 350 degree oven for 30 minutes or so, depending on the kind and thickness of the fish.* Fish should just begin to flake with a fork.

Garnish with freshly minced parsley.

* In testing this recipe with 1-inch thick halibut fillets, the fish was cooked in 20 minutes, registering 130 degrees on an instant read thermometer. If you use fillets that have been frozen, be sure to press them well with paper towels top and bottom to remove all excess moisture. Otherwise the fish will water down the sauce too much. Almost any fish works well in this dish except some kinds of sole. They turn gelatinous when baked.

2 tablespoons olive oil
2 cloves garlic, minced
1 medium onion, chopped
1 bunch green onions, chopped
2 stalks celery with leaves, chopped
4 small carrots, peeled and sliced
1 pound fresh spinach, washed and finely chopped
2 8-ounce cans tomato sauce
Coarse salt and freshly ground black pepper, to taste
1 bunch parsley, preferably flat-leaf, finely minced, reserve 2 tablespoons for garnish
2 1/2 pounds fresh fish fillets—red snapper, halibut, salmon, etc.
....
Optional: 3 large red or russet potatoes, peeled, cut into wedges

1 1/2 cups sugar
1 1/2 cups water
Grated peel of grapefruit
1 large ripe grapefruit, peeled and cut into segments
2 cups freshly squeezed grapefruit juice with pulp

GRAPEFRUIT SORBET

Heat sugar and water and bring to a boil, stirring to scrape down sugar crystals from the side of the pot. Simmer for 5 to 10 minutes. Remove from heat and cool to room temperature.

Place grapefruit peel and grapefruit in a food processor and purée. Add the juice at the end and pulse once or twice. Add the cooled sugar syrup and pulse to combine.

Freeze according to directions for your ice cream maker, or freeze in ice cube trays and process in a food processor just before serving to break up the chunks.

Makes approximately 2 quarts.

FRESH GREEN BEAN AND SHALLOT SALAD

This recipe was developed by Alma Lach, my cooking mentor in Chicago. She devised this simple-to-prepare salad when she was trying to lose some weight after teaching too many French-cooking classes!

Cook the green beans in a large pot of salted boiling water until bright green and crisp-tender, about 3 minutes. Immediately plunge into a bowl of ice water to stop the cooking, then blot dry with paper towels. Cut the beans into 1/2-inch lengths and reserve in a medium-sized bowl.

Combine the ingredients for the dressing in a glass measuring cup and reserve.

When ready to toss the salad, stir the dressing thoroughly. Spoon 2/3 of the dressing over the beans and toss well. Place the beans in a serving bowl. Spoon the remaining dressing over the reserved tomatoes and toss gently to combine. Arrange the tomatoes around the perimeter of the serving dish. Serve immediately.

Serves 6 to 8.

DM

1 pound fresh green beans, cleaned
1 pint cherry tomatoes, washed and halved

········

DRESSING
1/4 cup rice wine vinegar
1/4 cup water
1 tablespoon sugar
1 teaspoon coarse salt
Freshly ground black pepper, to taste
2 tablespoons minced shallots
1 tablespoon freshly minced parsley

ORIENTAL SEARED BEEF WITH VEGETABLES

2 New York steaks (boneless strip loin) about 10 to 12 ounces each, trimmed of all fat

2 tablespoons light soy sauce, such as Kikkoman

3 tablespoons sake wine or dry sherry

3 tablespoons beef broth

2 tablespoons rice vinegar

1 large clove garlic, finely minced

3 quarter-sized, unpeeled ginger slices, finely minced

4-inch length daikon radish, peeled

1/2 English cucumber

6 scallions

1/2 orange or red bell pepper

3 ears corn on the cob, fresh or frozen, cooked until just tender

4 to 5 ounces fresh mushrooms, mixed types if possible, such as oyster, shiitake, boletus

3 to 4 cups broccoli flowerets, stems trimmed to 1/2 inch, barely cooked

My dental hygienist is a native of Japan. She came to the U.S. to attend college, met and married an American, and now eats an assortment of western and oriental foods. In a Japanese home-style cookbook she lent me, I found a method of preparing beef which I found appealing and relatively low in fat and calories. I've mixed a bit of both Japanese and Chinese technique here. The recipe requires either an extremely hot barbecue grill or an indestructible cast-iron pan. The beef is "blackened" much like in Cajun cooking but without the same seasonings.

Begin by searing the beef. Heat a medium-sized cast-iron pan (the porcelainized finish on Le Creuset's "blackening" pans will also take the heat) until it is *very* hot. This can take 10 minutes over high heat on some ranges. Alternatively, build a very hot charcoal fire and wait for it to turn to grey ashes before cooking. Do not add any oil or butter to the pan. With the vent on high or the windows open - smoke *is* going to roll! - drop the trimmed beef into the pan or on the grill. Cook until a nearly black crust has formed. This should take about 2 minutes if the pan or grill is truly hot. Turn and "blacken" the other side and remove to a plate to cool. The meat is intended to be very rare in the middle. To protect counter surfaces, allow the pan to cool for 10 minutes before moving it off the range.

While the beef is cooling, prepare the dipping sauce and vegetables. For the dipping sauce, mix together the soy, wine, broth, vinegar, garlic, and ginger. Thinly slice the radish; slice the cucumber a bit thicker for better texture; draw a sharp knife lengthwise through the white portion of the scallions to form a scallion "flower"; thinly slice the pepper; cut the corn into "coins" about 1/4 inch thick; cut the various mushrooms into thumbnail-sized chunks; pat the broccoli dry with paper towels if it is wet.

Arrange an assortment of vegetables in an attractive pattern on each dinner plate. Slice the beef horizontally through the middle, across the grain, so that you have two pieces, each with a crusty side. Lay the crusty side down and slice strips about 1/8 to 1/4-inch thick. Arrange these on the plate with the vegetables. Stir up the dipping sauce and place some into a small ramekin or tiny bowl for each person.

Note: This is a perfect "do ahead" meal. Everything can be prepared a day or two in advance and the plates arranged just before serving.

Serves 6.

RICOTTA AND LINGONBERRY CHOCOLATE DACQUOISE

This is an elegant and texturally exciting way to end a low calorie meal. I have borrowed a technique of Maida Heatter's in which she beats ricotta cheese in a food processor until smooth and velvety. The ricotta is then combined with crisp chocolate meringues and tart lingonberries for a great taste sensation.

Preheat oven to 225 degrees. In a food processor work bowl fitted with the metal blade, place the almonds, both sugars, the cornstarch, and the cocoa. Process until finely blended. In a separate bowl, beat the egg whites with the cream of tartar until firm peaks have formed. (This will work best if the egg whites are at room temperature.)

Place the beaten egg whites in a large bowl for easy folding. Sprinkle one third of the nut mixture onto the egg whites and with broad strokes gently fold the nut mixture into the egg whites. Continue adding the nut mixture, one third at a time, until all is incorporated into the egg whites. Do not worry if a bit of egg white still shows, it is always better to underbeat a bit than to overbeat.

Butter and flour nonstick cookie sheets. Trace as many 3-inch rounds on the cookie sheets as possible. Using a #4 plain pastry tip pipe out a continuous circle, for each meringue, beginning in the center of the 3-inch round. If you do not have a pastry bag, then spoon the meringue mixture on the 3-inch rounds. This can also be done on 3-inch rounds of parchment that have been greased. The meringues should be approximately 1/3-inch thick.

Bake the meringue rings for approximately 1 1/2 hours until they are just barely soft in the center. Immediately place on racks to cool.

In the meantime, place the ricotta cheese and the honey in the workbowl of a food processor fitted with a metal blade. Process for one full minute until the texture is completely smooth. Refrigerate until ready to use.

When ready to serve, place one meringue round on each plate. Using half of the ricotta mixture, divide it among the 7 meringues. Spread it to the edge of the meringues. Then place a generous teaspoon of lingonberry preserves on top. Place another meringue on top and cover each meringue again with the ricotta and lingonberry preserves. Serve at once.

Makes 7 servings.

2 ounces blanched almonds, toasted, then finely chopped
1/2 cup superfine sugar
3/4 cup powdered sugar
1 tablespoon cornstarch
2 tablespoons unsweetened cocoa
4 egg whites (1/2 cup)
1/2 teaspoon cream of tartar
. . . .
15 to 16 ounces skim milk ricotta cheese
2 tablespoons honey
1/2 cup lingonberry preserves

BOWL DAY BASH

What are four non-football-watching cooks doing planning a menu for Superbowl Sunday??? Trying to help YOU entertain your friends, that's what!!!

Spicy Pecans
•
Shrimp Poached in Beer with Cajun Mayonnaise
•
Layered Fajita Salad
•
Bacon-Sour Cream Skillet Cornbread
•
Linebacker Moonpies

Dan has prepared some Spicy Pecans for munching during the first half.

We suggest you prepare all the food ahead of time, enjoy the first half, then put everything out buffet style and let your guests help themselves. The bread can be prepared and finished just before the start of the game or baked a few days ahead, frozen and reheated on low heat in the oven while you are absorbed in the game.

The Layered Fajita Salad takes some preparation, but all of it can be done ahead of time. Lettuce, black beans, cooked chicken, guacamole, and cheese are layered and then topped with a sour cream / rice mixture and salsa. Pass the tortilla chips!!!

Shrimp Poached in Beer with Cajun Mayonnaise and Dan's Bacon-Sour Cream Skillet Cornbread accompany the salad.

Giant Linebacker Moonpies are perfect for celebrating, or bemoaning, the end of the game! They are huge chocolate sandwich cookies that are refrigerated or frozen until serving time. Kathleen says they can be cut into smaller portions if you aren't a linebacker or don't eat like one!

Enjoy the day and we all certainly hope YOUR team wins!!

Georgia M. Vareldzis

6 tablespoons unsalted butter

4 teaspoons Tabasco

1 pound whole pecans

1 tablespoon sugar

1 1/2 teaspoons coarse salt

SPICY PECANS

Preheat oven to 350 degrees. Place butter on a large cookie sheet with sides. Place in oven for about 5 minutes to melt the butter. Remove from oven and stir in the Tabasco. Add the pecans to the pan and sprinkle them with the sugar and salt. Stir well to coat all the pecans. Place back in the oven and bake for 30 minutes stirring two to three times during the baking. Remove from the oven and drain in a colander. There will be some excess butter. Save it if you like—it is great for sautéeing. Allow pecans to cool.

Serves 10 to 12 armchair quarterbacks.

1 1/2 pounds shrimp (41 to 50 per pound)

....

16 ounces beer

2 cloves garlic, peeled, left whole

1 teaspoon coarse salt

1 bay leaf

1 teaspoon cumin seeds

1 teaspoon coriander seeds

3 small, dried hot red peppers, crushed with seeds

Juice of 1/4 lemon

1 tablespoon chopped fresh cilantro

SHRIMP POACHED IN BEER WITH CAJUN MAYONNAISE

Wash the shrimp, leaving the shells intact. Drain well. In a medium sauté pan, add the beer and remaining ingredients. Bring to a boil, then add the shrimp. When the shrimp turn pink, cook for one minute longer, then remove with a slotted spoon and reserve. Let the beer mixture cool. Add back the shrimp and refrigerate for at least 4 hours. Remove 20 minutes before serving and accompany with the Cajun Mayonnaise. Let the guests do the peeling.

Serves 10 to 12.

DM

3 extra-large egg yolks, at room temperature

2 tablespoons rice vinegar

1/2 teaspoon coarse salt

1 tablespoon Cajun seasoning blend

1 cup olive oil

Juice of 1/2 lemon

1 tablespoon boiling water

CAJUN MAYONNAISE

In the workbowl of a food processor fitted with the metal blade, add the egg yolks. Pulse to combine, then add in the vinegar, salt, and Cajun seasoning. Blend together. With the machine running, *slowly* add the oil in a thin stream through the feed tube. After all the oil is added, blend in the lemon juice and then the boiling water to keep the mayonnaise from separating. Refrigerate until ready to serve.

Makes 1 1/2 cups.

DM

LAYERED FAJITA SALAD

This salad was inspired by fajitas that I ate in a Mexican restaurant. It takes a little preparation, but it can be made ahead of time and served whenever you are ready. The chicken can be grilled or broiled in the oven. I use jalapeño or even serrano chilies in the guacamole and salsa. You can use milder chilies if you don't like hot dishes.

If you are cooking your own black beans, put them in a pot with the chicken stock and enough water to make 3 cups. Bring to a boil. Add the piece of onion, cumin, and oregano. Simmer, covered with the lid slightly ajar, until tender but not mushy. (It takes about 1 to 1 1/2 hours.) Drain and rinse with cool water. Set aside. If using canned beans, place in a pot without draining and add the cumin, oregano, bay leaf, and thyme. Cook about 15 minutes over low heat. Set aside to cool, draining if there is any excess liquid.

Cook the rice in water or the chicken broth and onion. You need 2 1/4 cups liquid for 1 cup raw rice. Set aside to cool.

To roast the peppers, char over a flame or under the broiler until they are completely blackened. Put in a plastic bag for 10 minutes. Remove and scrape off the skin and remove the seeds under cold running water. One-third of the chopped peppers is for the guacamole and as much of the rest as you like for the salsa. Divide and reserve.

Prepare the guacamole by combining the avocados, white onion, lemon juice, cilantro, chopped tomato, and one-third of the chopped chilies. Set aside. It can be refrigerated at this point until needed.

To make the salsa, combine the tomatoes, onion, garlic, cilantro, and as much of the remaining chilies as you like. If you don't want too much "heat" in your salsa, use less. Chill until ready to use.

Brush the chicken breasts with the olive oil/oregano mixture and grill or broil until they are browned and cooked. Allow to cool to room temperature, then slice into 1/2-inch chunks.

Shred the lettuce very fine and begin assembling the ingredients together. I like to use a 5-quart straight-sided glass bowl for this salad because it looks as good as it tastes when you can see the layers and all of the colors.

Layer the salad as follows: shredded lettuce, black beans, cheese, chicken pieces, guacamole. Spread 1 cup of the salsa over the top. Be sure to spread the ingredients out to the edge of the bowl, so all servings will have equal amounts of all the ingredients. Mix the sour cream and rice together. Spread over the top of the salad, covering completely. Put the remaining salsa in the middle of the sour cream layer. Garnish the sides with the sliced olives and sliced green onions. Serve the tortilla chips on the side.

1/2 cup black beans or 1 15-ounce can black beans
1 can (14.5-ounce) chicken broth
1/2 small onion
1 tablespoon ground cumin
1 tablespoon dried oregano
1 bay leaf
1/2 teaspoon thyme

. . . .

1 cup long-grain cooked rice (you may cook the rice in chicken broth with a little onion to give it more flavor)

. . . .

2-3 jalapeño peppers, roasted, cleaned, finely chopped

. . . .

GUACAMOLE
2 ripe avocados, peeled and mashed
1 tablespoon finely chopped white onion
1 tablespoon lemon juice
2 tablespoons minced fresh cilantro
1 medium ripe tomato, chopped very fine

. . . .

SALSA
2 large ripe tomatoes, peeled, seeded and diced
1/2 large white onion, chopped very fine
1 clove garlic, minced
1 bunch cilantro leaves, minced

. . . .

4-6 boneless chicken breasts (2-3 whole ones, cut in half)
1/4 cup olive oil with 1 teaspoon dried oregano mixed in
1/2 small head of lettuce, shredded
4 ounces sharp cheddar cheese, grated
1 pint sour cream
1 can (2.25 ounces) sliced black olives
2 green onions, thinly sliced

. . . .

Tortilla chips

3 tablespoons honey

1 tablespoon or 1 package active dry yeast

1/2 cup warm water

1 cup sour cream, at room temperature

2 eggs, at room temperature

3 cups all purpose flour, approximately

1 1/2 cups white or yellow cornmeal

1 1/2 teaspoons salt

1 teaspoon chili con carne seasoning

12 slices bacon, cooked until crisp and crumbled

2 tablespoons finely diced onion for garnish

BACON-SOUR CREAM SKILLET CORNBREAD

Stir the honey and yeast into the warm water and allow to sit until foamy, about 5 minutes. Stir the sour cream and eggs into the yeast mixture.

Place the flour, cornmeal, salt, and chili con carne seasoning in the workbowl of a food processor and run the machine until the mixture is combined. (Alternatively, make the bread by hand or use a mixer following the manufacturer's instructions). Add the bacon to the flour and cornmeal mixture. With the machine running, slowly pour the liquids into the dry ingredients, allowing a dough ball to form, and rotate (knead) for 60 seconds. Add a little more flour if the mixture sticks and is reluctant to rotate.

Place the dough in a gallon size plastic bag, squeeze out all the air, and place a wire twist at the *top* of the bag so that the dough has room to expand. Allow to rise in a warm place until approximately doubled in size, probably 30 to 60 minutes.

Remove the dough from the bag and spread it in a heavy, 12-inch non-stick or well-greased skillet. Cover with lightly oiled plastic wrap and allow to rise until nearly doubled in size.

Preheat the oven to 375 degrees. Remove the plastic wrap from the dough, sprinkle with the diced onion, and bake until nicely browned. An instant-read thermometer should register at least 180 degrees, about 25 minutes.

Cut into wedges and serve warm.

Serves 10 to 12.

LINEBACKER MOONPIES

The great dessert cookbook writer, Maida Heatter, was one of the first to include a recipe for Moonpies, one of the world's LARGEST cookies, in one of her cookbooks. I have long wanted to play around and develop my own version of these delicious "monsters." And here they are—the perfect "he-man" sandwich cookie for the perfect occasion.

Sift all dry ingredients together and set aside. Preheat oven to 375 degrees. Cut aluminum foil to fit cookie sheets. Use as many sheets as you have, and then recover them with clean aluminum foil as necessary. (The recipe will probably require about five separate sheets.)

Cream the butter until fluffy. Add the sugar and cream again until blended. Add the vanilla and then the two eggs, beating until completely mixed. Add the sifted dry ingredients in three separate batches interspersed with the milk in two portions.

Measure the batter with a 1/4-cup measure onto the cookie sheets. Place only five cookies on each sheet. Round them slightly after they are placed on the cookies sheets so that they spread evenly.

Bake each sheet for 18 minutes until they feel firm to the touch. Remove from the oven. Let the cookies cool for one minute and then peel back the foil. Do not let them sit longer or they will stick! Allow to cool completely on racks.

Place the flour, cocoa, and instant coffee in a 1-quart saucepan. Whisk in the milk gradually. If quite lumpy, strain. Cook the mixture over medium heat, stirring constantly until it thickens. Add the salt and one tablespoon of the butter. Remove from heat and stir until the butter has melted. Set aside and allow to cool to room temperature.

In the meantime, cream the remaining butter with the confectioners' sugar and vanilla until fluffy. Gradually add the cooled chocolate mixture. When all is added, beat on high speed for a minute until light and fluffy. Fold in the toasted filberts and chocolate chips. If the filling seems a little too runny to sandwich between the cookies, refrigerate for 30 to 45 minutes until firm.

Match up cookies in pairs that are as close in size as possible. Place a heaping tablespoonful of filling on the bottom of one cookie. Spread it to about 1/2 inch from the edge. Put enough filling on to make the cookie sandwich about 1/2-inch thick. Press the top cookie down very lightly and place the filled cookies in the refrigerator until very well set. Before storing in the refrigerator or freezer, wrap each cookie individually. Refrigerate up to one week or freeze up to one month.

Makes 10 to 11 huge cookies.

K. T.

COOKIE
1 1/2 cups all-purpose flour
1 1/2 cups cake flour
1 1/2 teaspoons baking powder
1 1/2 teaspoons baking soda
3 teaspoons cream of tartar
1/2 teaspoon salt
1/2 cup unsweetened cocoa
6 ounces (1 1/2 sticks) unsalted butter
1 1/2 cups sugar
1 1/2 teaspoons vanilla
2 large eggs
1 cup milk

FILLING
1/3 cup flour
3 tablespoons unsweetened cocoa
1 teaspoon powdered instant coffee
1 1/4 cups milk
Pinch of salt
3/4 pound of butter (3 sticks), room temperature
3 cups confectioners' sugar
1 1/2 teaspoons pure vanilla
2/3 cups toasted, skinned (as well as possible) filberts, cut in large pieces
1 cup chocolate chips

STARTING OVER

**Double Baked
Gruyere Potates**

•

**"Gone South"
Refried Beans**

•

Twice-Cooked Pork

•

**Rhubarb Upside
Down Cake**

"*For better, for worse . . . for richer, for poorer . . . in sickness and in health" . . . . These are just some of the vows mouthed by people who so very frequently wind up saying "I'm better without you, worse with you . . . richer in animosity, poorer in alimony . . . sick of you, a healthy sign!" Truly, America has become a land of split personalities when it comes to marriage.*

Whatever one's point of view on marriage and divorce one thing hasn't changed: everyone needs to eat regularly. Accordingly, we have married (oops!) a few tasty ingredients in the hope that when the inevitable newly divorced friend calls in need of spiritual sustenance, you'll be able to do even better than offer condolences—you'll be armed with our Starting Over menu! Invite the hapless friend (and several happily married couples, to show you've a sense of humor) to a simple little dinner. Make no mention of your menu motive! When the divorced pal asks what he/she can bring, casually announce that a split (!) of nice champagne might be appropriate. Pretend that you don't hear any long pauses on the other end of the line. If pressed as to the precise menu, you'll remark that it'll be a little leftover buffet and nothing fancy. (In fact, your little leftover buffet has been cunningly planned to poke fun at the institution of divorce!)

Serve Double Baked Gruyere Potatoes, Refried Beans, Twice-Cooked Pork, and Rhubarb Upside Down Cake. If anyone remarks, suggestively, that it seems to be a strange menu mix, just allow as how you had the ingredients on hand and just needed to "stir things up." Most of all, be truly supportive of a friend in need—be certain to offer him "seconds." And, please, don't forget a really elegant and often overlooked touch at meal's end: pour a nice glass of port to serve with some stinky cheese. Just ensure that the port is vintage dated—for the marriage year, of course!

Dave Taggart

DOUBLE BAKED GRUYERE POTATOES

6 large baking potatoes
6 tablespoons butter
1 large clove garlic, minced
1 bunch green onions, thinly sliced
1/2 cup blanched, slivered almonds
3 sprigs fresh rosemary
1 cup sour cream
6 ounces Gruyere cheese, shredded
1 cup plain yogurt
1/4 cup milk
Salt and freshly ground black pepper, to taste
2 tablespoons seasoned bread crumbs
2 tablespoons grated Parmesan cheese

Pierce the potatoes with a knife before baking. Bake the potatoes at 400 degrees for about 1 hour. Set the cooked potatoes aside to cool for 5 to 10 minutes. Slice them lengthwise and scoop out the insides into a bowl, reserving the shells.

While the potatoes are baking, melt the butter in a skillet or sauté pan. Add the garlic, green onions, and almonds. Cook over medium heat until the onions are soft and turn translucent. Finely chop the rosemary and add to the onion mixture. Stir for a minute or two to coat with the butter. Remove from the heat and set aside.

Mash the potatoes in the bowl, add the onion mixture, sour cream, Gruyere, yogurt, milk, and salt and pepper to taste. Beat the mixture with a mixer or use the wire whisk attachment of a food processor until smooth. Place back into the potato skin shells. You can use a large star tube and pastry bag to make the filling decorative. Mix the bread crumbs and Parmesan together and sprinkle a spoonful over the potato filling.

Place in a 400 degree oven for about 15 to 20 minutes until the potatoes are nicely browned on top. The potatoes can be prepared the day before, stuffed, and placed in the refrigerator until you are ready to bake them. They will take a little longer to cook.

Serves 8 to 12.

"GONE SOUTH" REFRIED BEANS

1 28-ounce can plain refried beans
1 large clove garlic, minced
1/4 cup minced onion
1/4 cup grated dry cheese, such as dry jack or quality Parmesan
1 canned chili chipotle, minced, plus 1 tablespoon of the sauce from the can*
1 green onion, finely sliced, for garnish

If you have spent a tough day listening to your friend's woes of being in Divorce Court you may not be up to "starting over" with dried beans, lard, seasonings, and several hours to make your own refried beans. Luckily your favorite market has the garden variety in cans. Turn ordinary canned refried beans into something more exciting by following these simple instructions!

In a heavy 2-quart saucepan, heat all the ingredients together until the beans are bubbly. If they are quite liquid, cook them, uncovered, until they have dried out a bit. Taste for seasoning, and add more chilies and/or sauce if you want more spice.

*Note: Chile chipotle refers to smoke-dried jalapeno. It has both the "heat" you would expect and a pleasant smokiness. You may find it in better supermarkets; if not, check where specialty Mexican foods are sold. They are usually found canned in "adobo" sauce, a dark tomato and vinegar sauce. "Herdez" is a commonly found brand.

Serves 6 to 8.

TWICE-COOKED PORK

This is a traditional dish of the Szechwan province. The pork is "twice-cooked" for added flavor and tenderness. Serve this full-flavored stir-fry with steamed white rice.

Freeze the pork for 30 minutes to make for easier slicing. In the meantime, mix the marinade ingredients together in a shallow bowl. Clean the leek and trim off the bottom. Cut the white and light green part of the leek into matchstick pieces. Clean the pepper and julienne. Place the leek, pepper, garlic, and ginger in a bowl and reserve. Combine the seasonings and set aside. Combine the cornstarch mixture and set aside.

Slice the meat into 1 1/2-inch long julienne.

Heat a wok over high heat, add the oil and heat to 350 degrees. Deepfry the pork just until it is no longer pink. Remove with a slotted spoon and let drain in a colander set over a plate to catch the excess oil. Remove all but 2 tablespoons of the oil. When the oil is hot stir-fry the leek, green pepper, garlic and ginger for 1 to 2 minutes. Stir the seasoning mixture, add to the wok, and heat through. Add the pork and stir-fry an additional minute. If the sauce needs to be thickened, stir the cornstarch mixture and add a small amount to the wok. (You should not need all of it.) Stir-fry an additional 30 seconds, then serve on a heated platter.

Serves 6 as part of a Chinese meal.

* I use Koon Yick Wah Kee brand chili sauce, which contains chili, onion, lemon, sweet potato, and vinegar.

DM

MARINADE
1 tablespoon soy sauce
1 1/2 tablespoons pale, dry sherry
1/4 teaspoon sugar
2 teaspoons cornstarch
....

1 pound boneless pork shoulder, fat left on
1 leek
1 large green pepper
1 large clove garlic, minced
1 teaspoon minced fresh ginger
....

SEASONINGS
1/2 teaspoon sugar
1 1/2 teaspoons soy sauce
2 teaspoons dry sherry
1 teaspoon chili sauce*
2 tablespoons Hoisin sauce
3 tablespoons chicken stock
....

1 teaspoon cornstarch
1 tablespoon water
....

2 cups peanut or corn oil for frying

RHUBARB UPSIDE DOWN CAKE

5 cups of rhubarb cut into 1-inch pieces

....

1 1/2 cups granulated sugar

1/2 cup water

1 teaspoon red food color, optional but prettier

6 large egg yolks

1 cup plain yogurt

2 teaspoon real vanilla extract

3 cups cake flour, unsifted

1 1/4 cup firmly packed dark brown sugar

1 1/2 tablespoons baking powder

1/4 teaspoon salt

12 tablespoons unsalted butter, softened

....

2 cups sour cream

Finely chopped zest of 1 medium orange

1 teaspoon cinnamon

2 tablespoons confectioners' sugar

Rhubarb is spring! It is one of the few vegetables whose season and availability has not been extended. This upside-down cake is a new version of a cake that Mom and I used to make each spring. We originally found the recipe in the CHICAGO TRIBUNE. It called for using a boxed white cake mix. Well, horrors, I couldn't do that! So I have devised a very tasty yogurt-brown sugar cake. When Diane tasted it she said she would love creme fraiche as a sauce. Be my guest; it would be great. The rest of us felt that the sour cream sauce is easy and excellent.

Preheat oven to 350 degrees. Spray a 9 x 13 baking dish with a nonstick food release or grease well. Arrange the rhubarb pieces evenly in the bottom of the pan.

Bring the sugar and water to a boil in a small saucepan. Add the red food color and set aside.

Blend the egg yolks, 1/4 of the yogurt, and the vanilla together. Place the dry ingredients in a large mixing bowl and blend at low speed. Add the softened butter and the remainder of the yogurt and beat at medium speed for about 1 1/2 minutes until well blended and smooth. At low speed, add the egg yolk mixture in three additions, beating completely after each. Pour and spread over the rhubarb. The batter will be thick. Pour the warm sugar syrup over the cake. Bake for approximately 50 minutes. Test the cake in several places with a cake tester to be sure all areas come out clean.

While the cake is baking, make the sauce. Blend the sour cream with the remaining ingredients and set aside. The sauce is best if cool but not ice cold.

When the cake is done, remove from oven and allow to cool for 10 minutes. Place a serving tray or large platter over the top and turn the cake over. Carefully remove the baking pan as it and the sugar syrup are hot. Allow the cake to cool for another 15 to 20 minutes before cutting and serving.

*T*he cake can be made in advance, but I do think it is best when served warm. I have found that the individual pieces of cake can be rewarmed nicely in a microwave – about 1 minute at medium power.

Serves 12.

K. T.